D1486014

ERNEST BEVIN
AND
THE FOREIGN OFFICE 1932-1969

SIR RODERICK BARCLAY, G.C.V.O., K.C.M.G.

ERNEST BEVIN
AND
THE FOREIGN OFFICE 1932–1969

LONDON
1975

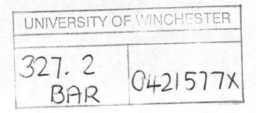
Printed in Great Britain by
Butler & Tanner Ltd, Frome and London

TO
JEAN

CONTENTS

ILLUSTRATIONS

(between pages 84 and 85)

PREFACE

W HEN my father was eighty-seven he wrote, for private circulation, some memoirs recalling scenes from his Victorian childhood and describing other aspects of his long life. These were read with much interest by friends and relations, and I recently decided that although I could not cover the same span of years I would try to follow his example. In doing so I had in mind primarily children, grandchildren and other members of my family, but since in the course of my diplomatic career I had naturally come into contact with many well-known and interesting personalities it occurred to me that what I wrote might appeal to a rather wider circle. Turning the pages of our visitors' book one can find the signatures of half a dozen foreign secretaries and a large assortment of other Cabinet ministers, not to mention ambassadors, admirals, field marshals, bishops and many others who have made their mark in one field or another. There are also the signatures of four queens and three kings who came to meals in our various houses.

Although in the first chapter and elsewhere there is a certain amount about myself, the main character in these pages is undoubtedly, as the title indicates, Ernie Bevin, by a long way the most remarkable of my various chiefs. I have not set out to give a full account of his last years and I have made no attempt to examine in detail his achievements as Foreign Secretary. My purpose was rather to describe some of my experiences while working with him, and in so doing to seek to give an impression of his character, gifts and personality. It seemed to me that this might be of some value, since there were few people who were as close to him as I was during the last two years of his life—and there are even fewer who are still alive today. The treatment of some of the other personalities discussed is still more fragmentary, and I fear rather superficial. To some extent I have tended to measure other politicians against him.

I have been told that if I want to appeal to a wider public I should be indiscreet, emphasise the personal weaknesses of the great, and in general adopt a strident tone. I have not followed this advice, chiefly, I suppose, because it would be contrary to my natural inclinations. I can only hope that in spite of my old-fashioned approach the reader may find something to interest and entertain him in these modest sketches.

Most of what I have written is based on memory and it may be that as a result an occasional error has crept in. If so I apologise in advance. I have never kept a proper diary, though I did make an attempt to record my doings during the first few months after I became Private Secretary to Ernie Bevin—and also during the last dramatic weeks of my time in France in June 1940. I have also occasionally been able to draw on letters written from abroad to my wife.

I have read most of the memoirs or diaries of former colleagues in the Diplomatic Service which have been published in recent years, and reference is made to one or two of these in the text. I have also read a good many political or military memoirs covering the period but have not thought it necessary to list or mention these individually. I have reread a number of the speeches made by Ernest Bevin or Herbert Morrison in the period 1949–51 but the confidential documents from this period are unfortunately not available for study.

It remains to thank those without whose assistance this book would never have appeared. I am particularly grateful to Julian Shuckburgh whose expert but kindly advice has been invaluable. Michael Wilford of the Foreign Office has read some sections and has confirmed or rectified my recollections of some of the experiences we shared, and to him, too, I am most grateful. I am glad to pay tribute to the efficient and cheerful secretarial assistance of Jean Edelsten. And finally I am indebted to various members of my family for encouragement and help, not least to my wife who took part in so many of the events here described—and one of whose drawings is reproduced as plate 1.

AUTOBIOGRAPHICAL

THIS book is basically about various eminent people for whom or with whom I worked, rather than about myself. It may, however, help to set the stage for what follows if I first give some account of my career in the Diplomatic Service, and before doing this I should perhaps also supply a few details about my family and upbringing. I realise that these may not be of great interest to the general reader, and some may therefore prefer to skip the rest of this chapter and move straight on to Ernie Bevin.

When, as I frequently have to do these days, I complete one of those irritating questionnaires beloved by immigration authorities, I write down 'Date of Birth: 22 February 1909. Place of birth: Kobe, Japan'. Kobe requires a little explanation, but first I must go back a little.

My father, Joseph Gurney Barclay, was born in 1879, the third son of Robert and Ellen Barclay of High Leigh, Hoddesdon. My grandfather was a banker, having joined his father as a partner in the family firm, which was then known as Barclay, Bevan, Tritton & Co., at the age of twenty-three. The family connection with banking goes back for well over two hundred years. It is not possible to establish with certainty in which year my four-times-great-grandfather, John Barclay, went into the firm of his grandfather, John Freame, but the latter had been carrying on banking business at the sign of the Black Spread Eagle in Lombard Street since before the year 1700, and John's older half-brother, James, had become a partner in 1736. Their father, David, had been the first member of the family to establish himself in business in London. Before that the Barclays had lived for several hundreds of years in Aberdeenshire, and latterly at Ury, near Stonehaven.

In the seventeenth century the Barclays had become Quakers and in this they resembled their future banking associates, the Bevans and Trittons, and indeed most of the families whose businesses were finally merged to form Barclay & Co. Ltd—the Gurneys, Tukes, Seebohms, Birkbecks, Backhouses and so on. The most remarkable among my Quaker forebears was Robert (the father of the above-mentioned David) who became celebrated as the author of the 'Apology', described as 'an explanation and vindication of the principles and doctrines of the people called Quakers'. This was a best-seller in its day, being translated into five languages from the original Latin, and being commended by Voltaire among others. Robert, who was at the same time a large Scottish landowner and non-resident Governor of the American state of East New Jersey, became a close friend of the Duke of York, later James II, whom he sought to influence in favour of religious toleration, with good results at least as far as the Quakers were concerned.

My grandfather had been brought up as a Quaker but became a member of the Church of England when he married Elizabeth Ellen Buxton. She was a granddaughter of Sir Thomas Fowell Buxton, who, following on from Wilberforce, did much to secure the passage through Parliament of the legislation abolishing slavery throughout the British Empire. Thomas Fowell had married Hannah Gurney of Earlham, a sister of Elizabeth Fry, the prison reformer. In addition to the banking connection, therefore, the family had a strong tradition of piety and of devotion to good causes, many of which they supported with great generosity.

Another characteristic was a strong addiction to field sports, in particular shooting. My great-grandfather is said to have been a very good shot but to have lost his enthusiasm when he saw his father blow a hole through the brim of his Quaker hat while recharging his muzzle-loader. The old gentleman was apparently quite unmoved. My grandfather used to shoot at his home at High Leigh and on his Higham estate in Suffolk, while every summer he took the family to Scotland where he rented a series of grouse moors before finally buying Tarvie, in Perthshire. My father was one of the keenest and best shots in the family.

My father followed his eldest brothers to Harrow, where he was Head of his House, and then went to Trinity, Cambridge, where he got a first in Natural Science. He then went into the Bank at Cambridge, where he was to work for the next eight years, interrupted by a leisurely trip round the world. When he was twenty-six he married Gillian, daughter of Henry Birkbeck of Westacre, a Director of Barclays Bank, whose family had also been Quakers and who were at least as keen on sport of all kinds as the Barclays. I was always given to understand that one of the reasons why my Birkbeck grandfather gave up being a Quaker was because he wished to wear a pink coat out hunting—which was of course frowned on by strict members of the Society of Friends. Whereas my Barclay grandfather elected to have prunes for lunch every day at the bank, 'Old Harry'—as he was known to many friends—had a weakness for oysters and *foie gras*, and his drink all through lunch was port. They both lived to be nearer eighty than seventy and I saw my Birkbeck grandfather at seventy-five shooting as well as ever, so his less abstemious diet seemed to suit him.

My parents, after three years of ideally happy married life in Cambridge, decided, to the admiration of some and the consternation and surprise of others, to go off as missionaries to Japan. They had prematurely come to the conclusion that they were unlikely to have any children, but a year later I was born. My mother never fully recovered and died when I was three months old. By all accounts she was a person of particular grace and charm as well as of deep religious faith.

I was brought back to England in the care of a nurse, supervised by my grandmother and an aunt. My father decided to go on working in Japan, and I went back there with him, achieving the then unusual distinction of having been round the world before I was eighteen months old. I was a much travelled child, for I returned home again across Siberia before I was three, causing a slight flurry by biting a piece out of a glass in Moscow. I have no recollection of these early travels, but I do remember quite well my third trans-Siberian journey which we undertook when I was five. My chief interest in life then was trains, and to spend fourteen days in one—for that was what the journey took in those leisurely days—was my idea of a good life. I can still picture the wood-burning engine with its bulbous funnel, and I remember too playing endlessly with a little Russian girl with whom I was of course quite unable to converse. On arrival at Liverpool Street I remarked to my father that it would be rather fun to start back again.

I have been told that I was a good-natured and easy-going

child, and during that lonely period I must have been some consolation to my father. If so I was amply repaid by his affectionate interest in all my doings down to this day, and he has remained an important influence throughout my life.

When I was six my father married again, and I returned to Japan until finally sent back to preparatory school in this country. Having always had an English nurse or governess my knowledge of Japanese was never extensive, though I still remember a few words and phrases.

Like my father I went to Harrow and Trinity, Cambridge. At Harrow, after a rather shy start, I enjoyed myself greatly, became in due course a school monitor, and without undue exertion won a large number of prizes and a leaving scholarship in Modern Languages. I was an enthusiastic but not particularly talented player of all games, achieving modest distinction at football and fives. There were many of my cousins in the school, and in particular in our House, and on arrival I appeared in the lists as Barclay Sextus. I was still only Barclay Minimus when I got into the Sixth Form.

At Trinity I led a very varied life, doing a moderate amount of work, playing an assortment of games and joining a variety of clubs and societies, sporting, philanthropic and religious. I only managed to get a Second Class (Division I) in both parts of the Modern Language Tripos, partly no doubt because I spent a good deal of time on (literal) wild goose chases on The Wash and other such time-consuming activities, and partly because, when I should have been spending my long vacations improving my languages in France or Germany, I went climbing or shooting and fishing in Scotland.

When I left Harrow my reply to enquiries about what I intended to do in life was that I hoped to go into the Bank. I had in fact been up for an interview with the Chairman of Barclays, Sir F. C. Goodenough and, I believe been approved. At Cambridge, however, I became attracted by the idea of the Diplomatic Service. I fancy that the first time I seriously thought about it was when our Director of Studies said to all the budding Trinity modern linguists, 'I suppose a lot of you young men think that you are going to pass into the Diplomatic Service. I can assure you that none of you stand a chance.'

On going down from Cambridge I began to work very much harder than hitherto in preparation for the Diplomatic Service examination. In those days this was a very comprehensive and somewhat daunting test, requiring not only a pretty high standard of French and German but an extensive knowledge of a variety of other subjects, including European history, economics, current affairs and even 'everyday science'. I spent the next year mostly abroad, but partly at a crammer in London. When in due course the examination results were announced I was placed seventh out of seventy, but there had been only three vacancies so I was among the unsuccessful. I now had to decide whether to try again, or to accept an appointment to some other branch of the Government Service, or to do something quite different. It was not an easy decision, but I was reluctant to accept defeat, and fortified by the promise of further financial assistance from my father I decided to have another go.

The next year I spent partly at Cambridge and partly abroad, in Bonn, Dresden, Vienna, Paris and Wimereux. Here, staying with the famous Professor Martin, I overlapped with Terence Rattigan, whose experiences doubtless gave him the idea for *French Without Tears*, though the glamorous girls of the play were unfortunately not in evidence.

In April I had joined some Trinity friends on a 'reading party' (I do not know whether such things still take place) at Seatoller in the Lake District. Apart from work we went on various expeditions and on one of these I took two members of the party up a climb in Piers Ghyll on Scafell. I was leading and had reached an awkward spot when the piece of rock to which I was clinging broke away and I fell about forty feet on to a scree slope. We were roped, and if I had fallen any further either the next man on the rope would have held me or alternatively I would have pulled him off too. The other members of the party, who were not far away, joined my two climbing companions, and, having fetched a stretcher from Wasdale Head, they carried me down the mountain, no easy task and one which took till nightfall. I was exceptionally lucky, for though very badly cut and bruised, particularly on hands and face, I had suffered no major injury. A newspaper report, headed 'Almost a Tragedy', gave a graphic but not exaggerated account of the accident. After a fortnight in Keswick

Cottage Hospital I was able to go off and convalesce, and a week or two later Sir Harold Gillies, the eminent plastic surgeon, went to work on my face with such success that most people do not now notice the scars. Sad to say, neither of my two companions on the rope is alive today, one of them, Tim Bull, having been killed at Anzio after greatly distinguishing himself in the fighting in North Africa. Of the other members of the party, one, Sammy Hood,* became a distinguished colleague in the Foreign Office while a second, John Nicholson,† now sits beside me at Board meetings once a fortnight.

My accident had not set me back unduly and in July I took the Foreign Office examination again. Some six weeks later I was out shooting partridges at Westacre when a cousin rode up with a telegram of congratulations, for this time, to my relief and satisfaction, I had been successful.

I began work at the Foreign Office in October 1932, and was allocated to the Northern Department which handled relations with Russia, Poland, the Baltic States and Scandinavia. Nowadays new entrants to the Office have the advantage of admirably organised courses of instruction which give them an impression of how the Foreign Office and Whitehall machines operate. In 1932 there was nothing so sophisticated and you had to find out gradually for yourself.

In the course of the year I spent in Northern Department we had one period of considerable activity during the trial in Moscow of the Metro-Vickers engineers (who had been arrested on trumped-up charges of espionage) but the normal tempo was leisurely. I dealt primarily with Scandinavia, which meant that I was chiefly involved with fishery disputes. I also wrote a memorandum about Greenland, the ownership of which was then disputed by the Danes and Norwegians. When concluding, as I did, that the Danish claim was the stronger, I little thought that I should one day visit the country myself as the guest of the Danish Government.

In those days we did not begin work until the gentlemanly hour

* Viscount Hood, formerly a Deputy Under Secretary of State in the Foreign Office.

† Sir John Nicholson, Bart., former Chairman of Martins Bank and now Director of Barclays.

of 11 o'clock, the theory being that the registries would by then have sorted the morning telegrams and other mail and prepared the papers for the attention of the young gentlemen in the Departments. Somebody had to remain on duty at lunchtime, but if one had a luncheon engagement there was no difficulty about being out from one until three o'clock. Tea in our Department was a social occasion. Work stopped and an elderly 'departmental lady' came and presided over a lavish spread of scones and butter, biscuits, fruit cakes and chocolate cakes. The Head of our Department, Laurence Collier★ used to join us in the 'third room' and entertained the juniors with selections from his ample fund of anecdotes about some of the more eccentric characters in the Service. These sometimes took a long time to come out as he had a very bad stammer. It was considered permissible to go home at any time after 6 o'clock, but if there was a lot of work one might have to stay later. We worked every Saturday morning, which was frustrating, but on the other hand we were all entitled to two months' holiday a year and this was one of the attractions of the Service. The reverse of the medal was that the starting salary of a Third Secretary was only £275 a year, which meant that until he was sent abroad and received foreign and rent allowances it was impossible even for a bachelor to live on his pay.

After a year in London I was sent as Third Secretary to Brussels, where I remained for the next three years. I had meanwhile become engaged to be married to Jean Gladstone, and our wedding took place in London the following summer. Our mothers had been cousins and close friends, and I had stayed several times with Jean's family at Capenoch in Dumfriesshire. We had also met in Paris when she was at a finishing school, at May Week, and in London, so that by the time we got engaged we had come to know each other pretty well. We have lived ever since, in the words of the marriage service, 'in perfect love and peace together' and our partnership has been an exceptionally happy one.

My father-in-law, Sir Hugh Gladstone, as he later became, was a great figure locally, being Convenor of the County Council and subsequently Lord Lieutenant. He was a noted ornithologist and a particularly keen and good shot, so that we had certain interests

★ Later Sir Laurence Collier, Ambassador to Norway.

in common. He was a splendid Edwardian character who talked very fast into his drooping moustache, with the result that ladies sitting next to him at table found him very difficult to follow. During the last war, when he was approaching seventy, he went to stay, when grouse shooting, in a small hotel where he learnt that there would be nobody to pack for him, and since he had never in his life had to pack his own luggage, he sought Jean's advice on how to set about it! Many people on hearing the name Gladstone ask, 'Any relation to the Prime Minister ?' The answer in his case was first cousin twice removed.

Brussels in those days was a quiet and rather provincial capital. It had the merit of being marvellously cheap and we had a pleasant little house where we lived very comfortably. There, the following year, our eldest daughter, Gillian, was born. Meanwhile, we had been almost continuously in Court mourning. Shortly after my arrival King Albert was killed in a climbing accident; then, after a short gap, came the death of King George v; and finally Queen Astrid was killed when being driven by her husband, King Leopold. The Belgians were then, and indeed still are, extremely zealous mourners, and for many months Jean was expected to wear nothing but black. She was even supposed to wear a black veil whenever she went out. Practically all social activities involving the Diplomatic Corps came to an end, and as Belgium was then in the depths of the economic depression there was relatively little private entertainment by Belgians either. This did not greatly worry us. We enjoyed having numerous friends and relations to stay, and we returned for lengthy holidays in Scotland and elsewhere.

Meanwhile the European scene was gradually growing more sombre and Belgium was reluctantly involved in all the major political developments such as the German reoccupation of the Rhineland. We had a very small staff at the Embassy so that I had to set my hand to a variety of tasks and there were periods of considerable activity, though equally there were times when work in the Chancery was slack and life was leisurely.

In the autumn of 1936 I was posted back to the Foreign Office and joined the Central Department which then dealt with Germany and her relations with her neighbours—including of course Poland and Czecho-Slovakia—France and the Low Countries. I was to stay in this department for the next three and a half years, and though I did not myself handle the German papers, being primarily concerned with France, and, some of the time, with Belgium and Holland, I was well placed to observe the deepening crisis. It could not but be a depressing period as it became increasingly clear that sooner or later war with Germany was almost inevitable.

We had in succession three very able heads of our Department, Ralph Wigram, who was unfortunately taken ill and died not very long after my return, then William Strang,* and finally Ivone Kirkpatrick,† both of whom were in due course to become Permanent Under Secretary of State. The tempo in the Office had changed noticeably since my days in the Northern Department. We began work earlier and stayed later in the evening. The other members of the Department were less eccentric and more competent than most of my colleagues in Northern Department had been, and in spite of the pervasive atmosphere of frustration and gloom which then afflicted the whole Foreign Office, I found working in Central Department a rewarding and stimulating experience.

We were meanwhile comfortably established in a house in Walpole Street, where in 1937 our second daughter, Susan, was born. We thought ourselves rather hard up but nevertheless had a cook, a house-parlourmaid, a nanny and a nurserymaid.

I do not propose to embark on a discussion of Munich or of our policies generally in the immediate pre-war period, since this would involve straying far beyond the scope of the present volume. I accordingly pass on to my next appointment—in February, 1940—to the Embassy in Paris.

I was told that my selection for this post was to be regarded as a compliment, and so I suppose it was, but it was not the ideal moment to be establishing ourselves in Paris. No one, of course, could then foretell when the war in the West would flare up. A German invasion of the Low Countries which had seemed imminent in January had not materialised, but was surely bound to come, and though I did not then foresee that we should be forced to evacuate Paris less than four months later, we decided

* Later Sir William, then Lord Strang.
† Later Sir Ivone Kirkpatrick.

that it was not the moment to take the children there. Jean, who was expecting another baby in May, came with me for a few weeks and saw me comfortably established in a flat in the Avenue St Honoré d'Eylau, before returning to the family in Dumfriesshire. It was a good thing she did not stay, for our third daughter, Davina, was born on 9 May and on 16 May the rapidity of the German advance caused all the Embassy wives and families to be hurriedly despatched home. (I shall have more to say about my time at the Paris Embassy and the Fall of France in a later chapter.)

On returning to the Foreign Office at the end of June I was appointed to the newly created French Department. Here the work during the next few months was of particular interest. The presence in London of General de Gaulle and his followers gave rise to plenty of problems. We also had to decide how to treat the Vichy Government in France and to deal with the repercussions throughout the French Empire of the French collapse.

The late summer of 1940 was an exhilarating time to be working in London. Shortly after our return from France the decisive air battles began, and one frequently saw formations of aeroplanes high over Whitehall. I regard myself as having been very fortunate to have been on the spot and not at some distant Embassy that summer and during the blitz winter that followed.

During this period we had no regular home. The children were safely established with their grandparents in Scotland and Jean alternated between them and visits to me in the south. We stayed mostly with my father in Hertfordshire, whence she came up to work in the National Gallery canteen. During the blitz commuting became difficult and time-consuming, for one never knew quite how long one would spend sitting in a darkened train with a raid in progress. On the night of the great September fire in the City I was catching a train from Liverpool Street. The approach road was blocked with fires and fallen masonry and parts of the roof fell on our platform, so we were quite glad to pull out of the station. The red glow from the fires was clearly visible twenty miles away. For a time I had a small flat in Chelsea where we had one or two near misses from bombs. I later took to spending some nights in the Foreign Office basement, where quite a few members of the staff, including two senior Under Secretaries who had been bombed out, had now taken up residence.

Early in 1941 I was informed that I was being appointed to the Embassy in Washington. Jean and I had mixed feelings about going abroad at that time, but at least we now had had some experience of life in wartime Britain. Moreover, if we had got to go somewhere abroad there could be no more interesting destination than Washington. It was also clearly a good place for the children.

I was required to be in Washington by the end of April, and the first problem was how to get there. There was no question at that time of families going by air, and we eventually found ourselves at Liverpool, where, after a night disturbed by air raids, we boarded what looked to us to be a tiny ship in which to cross the Atlantic—the SS *Nerissa* of the Furness-Withy Line. Our initial briefing was not exactly cheering. We were never to let the children out of our sight, never to undress fully, and we must realise that if hit by a torpedo we were likely to go down in two minutes. Although by no means speedy we were to proceed unescorted and not in convoy. As we now know this was one of the worst periods for sinkings in the Atlantic of the whole war.

After fourteen days at sea on a course which had taken us within sight of Iceland and close to Greenland, we finally reached Halifax, and very thankful we were to get there. We had our share of alarms and had actually sighted a submarine, though at a considerable distance. For the first time on the voyage I had risked having a bath and was just drying myself when all the alarm bells started to ring. Jean, our nanny and I had arranged each to be responsible for one child, and I and my charge were inevitably a bit behindhand in bundling on warm clothes and reaching our boat station. However, after a period of suspense while we tried to judge whether the submarine was gaining on us or we were drawing away, the submarine disappeared and we could relax. Our poor little ship was sunk on the return journey and there were few survivors.

Halifax was still partly covered with snow when we landed, but when we eventually stepped out of our train at Washington we encountered a heat-wave—an early warning of the eccentricities of the Washington climate. The humid heat of the long summers is notorious, but I had not previously realised how severe the winters can be. In the course of the next three years I was to see forsythia in full flower weighed down by snow and to skate on frozen rivers and enjoy long toboggan runs with my eldest daughter down into Rock Creek Park.

We soon got ourselves established, in a comfortable house in Thirty-second Street, where the cardinals and blue jays used to enhance the pleasure of our patch of garden. In no time, too, we were caught up in the manifold activities of the Embassy. I shall have something to say of my new chief, Lord Halifax, in a later chapter.

Throughout my time in Washington my special responsibility was for Western European affairs, which meant primarily the problems of the French. From the outset, and throughout my stay, there was a sharp divergence of view between the Foreign Office and the State Department on the issues of the Free French versus Vichy, of Giraud and de Gaulle, on the 'deal with Darlan' after the landings in North Africa, and on what to do when French territory was liberated. Though I had seen enough of General de Gaulle in London to have some reservations about him and some of the members of his entourage I was nevertheless a firm believer in the Free French cause, and was convinced that American policy was shortsighted and wrong.

Unfortunately, not only the American Secretary of State, Cordell Hull, but President Roosevelt himself were violently anti de Gaulle, and as we now know, Winston too was on several occasions almost convinced that the General must be jettisoned. I should much like to have been present at some of the Churchill–de Gaulle confrontations, which, incidentally, evoked some of the former's classic comments. I suppose everyone knows his complaint about the cross of Lorraine being one of the heaviest of those he had to bear, but I still smile at the thought of, 'Can anyone tell me, what is the opposite of *Vive la France*?'

One of my special duties was to help the Free French Delegation, who were in a constant state of frustration if not fury over the American attitude. They were not recognised as a diplomatic mission and consequently had no right to send cypher telegrams, so that any confidential message to or from London had to be sent through our Embassy, which meant through me. There were occasions when I had to insist on toning down or rewriting the impassioned drafts brought to me by Monsieur Tixier, the Head of the Delegation, who was later to be a member of the first post-liberation French Government. He was succeeded by Monsieur Boegner, a son of the celebrated Pasteur Boegner, Head of the Protestant Church in France. A brother of his, also an ardent Gaulliste and a more rigid and orthodox character, was later for many years French Ambassador to the European Communities.

I could not always get Lord Halifax to share my pro-Free French sympathies and indeed he was often inclined to share the irritation of Winston and Roosevelt with General de Gaulle and to think that Anthony Eden and the Foreign Office were going too far in their opposition to the State Department.

The entry of the United States into the war meant a dramatic change in the Embassy's responsibilities. Some problems were eased by the fact that the Americans were now our allies, but in most respects the volume and complexity of our tasks were increased.

I well remember being called to the telephone at the end of lunch on the Sunday of Pearl Harbour and being told by William Hayter,* who was then Head of Chancery, that the President had just given the Ambassador the startling news of the Japanese bombardment. While he rang up the Foreign Office he asked me to inform the four local Commonwealth Ambassadors. When I gave the news to the New Zealander he replied, 'Splendid, now we'll soon polish off those . . . Japs.' Though I certainly did not anticipate the full extent of the disasters which were about to befall, I did not believe that things were going to be all that easy and said so. Some weeks later, after the fall of Singapore, the New Zealand Ambassador reminded me of this exchange, and ruefully admitted that he had somewhat misjudged the situation.

Not long after Pearl Harbour we received a top secret telegram which the Ambassador was instructed to decypher himself. In spite of enlisting the help of Lady Halifax he found this altogether too complicated and the Chancery were asked to take over. The message heralded the early arrival of Winston Churchill for the first of many top-level Anglo-American meetings.

One feature of this visit was the enormous fan-mail and the large assortment of Christmas presents sent to the Prime Minister

* Later Sir William, Ambassador to Moscow and now Warden of New College.

by American well-wishers. All the Embassy wives were roped in
to help deal with the letters, while in return there was a share-out
of the presents. Apart from the inevitable brandy and cigars and
such items as home-made cakes and jam our share included a
bath-mat in the form of a Union Jack and a lady's version of a
Trinity House Coat.

The work at the Embassy continued to be exacting but interesting, and I later got involved in working with the State Department, Pentagon, and our Service Missions on draft armistice
terms for Italy. Though there was not much time for relaxation,
life in Washington was in many ways enjoyable. We had many
close friends among the constantly expanding Embassy staff and
also among the members of the various British Missions, both
Service and civilian. We also received much hospitality from
American friends in the State Department and outside.

It was of course a difficult period in which to get to know the
country. Travel was complicated by 'gas rationing' and anyhow
there was too much work to make it possible to get away except
for very brief periods. I did, however, manage one official trip to
Kansas City, Denver, Salt Lake City and San Francisco, and
another to Atlanta and New Orleans, and there were more frequent visits to New York. Jean and the children twice went up
to stay with a friend in New Brunswick to escape from part of the
Washington summer, and the third year we rented a summer
cottage at Hyannis Port. I only had a fortnight's leave each year
so could not join them for long.

In September 1943 I flew back to England for a short visit.
Some of the time was devoted to a tour of factories, airfields, etc.,
arranged by the Ministry of Information, and I spent several days
at the Foreign Office. I also had a few days' leave and managed
to fit in a day's grouse driving with my father-in-law and one or
two days after partridges in the south. I returned to Washington
with a brace of partridges in my mackintosh pocket, which must
have been contrary to some regulation. I flew both ways in RAF
bombers and the journey was not exactly luxurious. On the way
out I began after a time to feel decidedly poorly, and noticed that
some of my fellow-travellers, who like me were lying on the floor
of the bomber, were also tossing about in apparent discomfort.
Eventually a member of the crew opened the cabin door and

surveyed us. 'Good Lord, we forgot to tell them,' he observed cheerfully, and it emerged that the reason for our plight was that we had not been told to put on the oxygen masks which were available, and which, owing to our altitude, were in fact now very necessary. Once we had done so and plugged in we soon felt very much better.

In the early summer of 1944 I was told that I was to return to the Foreign Office. After more than three years in Washington we were glad to be going home. We again travelled by sea, but this time we were on a Norwegian troopship which formed part of a heavily escorted convoy and we felt much more secure than we had done in the little *Nerissa*. There were about two thousand American troops on board, and our three girls soon became favourites, receiving endless presents of sweets, chewing-gum, coke, etc.

We were bound for Glasgow and as we sailed up the Clyde we heard the Scottish countryside being likened to that of almost every state in the Union. The appearance of girls waving on one or other bank caused such a rush to the rails on that side of the ship that she listed quite heavily and strict orders had to be given prohibiting such behaviour. We finally docked late on a Saturday night and were not allowed to go ashore until the next morning. Though our destination was only Dumfriesshire there were no trains all day, and Glasgow on a Sunday in wartime was not exactly gay. We finally boarded the night train for London which fortunately stopped at Dumfries. There we were met by a taxi, but owing to petrol rationing this was not allowed to take us more than fifteen miles and we had to turn out by the roadside with all our luggage and pile into a second taxi in order to complete the journey to my father-in-law's house. The grandparents were charmed by the three girls, and impressed by their capacity to consume large quantities of cold salmon and strawberries at 1 o'clock in the morning.

This was the period of the flying bomb, to which were shortly added the v2 rockets, so we decided to leave the children in Scotland for the time being. After various temporary expedients, however, we acquired a house on the edge of Hemel Hempstead which had belonged to an uncle of my wife. The v1 and v2 launching sites having in the meanwhile been over-run by the advancing allied armies, we were able to bring the children south and settle into the house which was to be our home for the next eight years. We had a large garden and a tennis court, ponies and dogs, and after the town life of Washington the girls were able to enjoy the pleasures of the English country. Here, in January 1947 our son, Joe, was born.

I had been posted to the newly created Personnel Department. It was a curious feature of the Foreign Office that until then the personnel questions of the Diplomatic Service had been handled by the Assistant Private Secretary to the Secretary of State, with the help of the so-called Chief Clerk and his Department, who were concerned primarily with pay and finance. Though my new job did not sound glamorous I was genuinely interested in personnel matters, and the expanding Department certainly had plenty of problems ahead. With the end of the war now in sight we could begin to work on the implementation of the 'Eden Reforms' (which had been announced in a White Paper published in 1943) and which provided, among other things, for the constitution of a unified Foreign Service, embracing the hitherto separate Diplomatic, Consular and Commercial Diplomatic Services. It was soon going to be possible to resume recruitment, and we had to decide by what methods this should be done. Finally there was the urgent task of providing staff for the posts in countries as they were liberated, which called for constant improvisation.

Before long I moved up to be Number Two in the Department, and in 1946 I became Head of it. It was a challenging job and at times a worrying one as we sought, with a mere handful of staff, to accomplish what is now done, doubtless more smoothly and professionally, by several hundred. A great deal of my time was inevitably taken up with interviews or selection boards and I frequently found myself having to go back to my papers after dinner, in which case I normally slept on a camp bed in my office.

Many of those who are now filling senior posts in the Diplomatic Service were recruited during that period, and in many cases I was probably the first person they met in the Foreign Office. I also had a hand in bringing into the Service a number of men who were over-age for the normal examination but who proved very valuable acquisitions, including Humphrey Trevelyan,* later to be Ambassador in Cairo and Moscow, and Dennis Greenhill,† till recently Permanent Under Secretary.

In the next chapter I shall recount how, to my surprise, I found myself translated from this job to be Principal Private Secretary to the Secretary of State, and since my period as Private Secretary is described in that and following chapters, I now jump to the autumn of 1951.

At one moment I was given to understand that on ceasing to be Private Secretary I might be required to go as Ambassador to Libya, but it was rightly decided that an Arabic-speaker was needed for that post, and in the end I was promoted instead to be an Assistant Under Secretary of State. I was to supervise the American Department, which looked after both North and South America, and also a number of technical Departments, Protocol, Consular, Claims, etcetera.

I had enough to do but was seldom hard-pressed unless it so happened that I was in addition keeping an eye on the work of some other Under Secretary who was away on leave. During one such period I was temporarily looking after the Far East, where there was as usual a good deal going on, and this resulted in my having on several occasions to go across to Number 10 to clear telegrams with Winston Churchill, who, in the absence through illness of Anthony Eden, was in charge of the Foreign Office. I had met him in Washington and on several social occasions when I was Private Secretary, but had not previously had to transact business with him. I usually found him sitting alone at the long green baize-covered table in the Cabinet Room. He was in full agreement with the Foreign Office on our Far Eastern policy at that period, so that my sessions with him were not difficult, but I always enjoyed hearing his comments, and there was always a sound reason for any drafting amendment which he made.

Also at this time I had a certain amount to do with the Minister of Defence, who was none other than the great Alex. I think everyone agrees that he was not a good Minister and he did not seem to enjoy the job, but one could not help being struck by his extraordinary personal charm. Later, when I was Ambassador in Brussels, I was to have further dealings with him—on the occasion

* Now Lord Trevelyan.
† Now Lord Greenhill.

of the fiftieth anniversary of the Battle of Paschendaele, and then he was completely master of the situation.

As Under Secretary for the Americas I had an opportunity, which I warmly welcomed, to go on a tour round South America as principal adviser to Lord Reading, then Minister of State at the Foreign Office. This so-called good-will mission was rather a rushed affair since we only spent about three days in each of the places we visited—Rio, Montevideo, Buenos Aires, Santiago and then Lima. There we parted, Lord Reading going off to the Far East while I went on to Bogota and Caracas before finally returning home via Washington, where I had a chance to compare notes with the State Department.

The tour involved a lot of speech-making which Lord Reading accomplished gracefully and well, and, inevitably much eating and drinking. Lord Reading was a teetotaller and firmly refused the champagne and whisky which were constantly being pressed on us at unsuitable times of the day—which made it almost impossible for me to do likewise without causing offence.

Before this I had not realised quite how different the countries of South America are one from another or how great is the contrast between the Pacific and the Atlantic coasts. I found the flight over the Andes an exciting experience, while the view of the great snow-covered peaks from among the roses and sweet peas in the gardens of Santiago made an indelible impression. So, of course, in quite a different way, did the Bay of Rio. The flight up from Cali to Bogota was fairly dramatic as we were most of the time in thick cloud, with occasional glimpses of jagged mountains which seemed uncomfortably close to our wing tips. It was a relief when we were landed safely at Bogota, though the altitude at once gave me a severe headache. We had not, incidentally, experienced the much greater height of La Paz where my daughter Davina and her husband were later to have a tour of duty.

In spite of its rather hurried nature I think our trip did some good, since a visit by a British Minister was then almost unheard of, and our hosts seemed duly gratified. The tour also gave us a chance to visit our various Embassies and talk to the staff, an experience which I was to find useful in my next job.

There had meanwhile been an important development in our private life. For two or three years we had realised that the designation of Hemel Hempstead as a New Town was bound before long to spoil the charms of our house which was destined to become engulfed by new building developments. We had therefore been on the lookout for something in the same general area which would suit us. After one or two disappointments we had an opportunity to buy a Queen Anne farmhouse, Great White End, near Latimer, which we fortunately took, and this has been our home ever since. We have never regretted the decision and most people agree that the house, with its rose-garden, barns and surrounding meadows has great charm. Here, as at High Firs, Jean's deeply engrained love of horses could have full play. The house had first been commended to us by a neighbour on the grounds that from the drawing room window she would be able to see the horses' heads looking out of their loose boxes, which is indeed the case. We received what would now seem a derisory sum for our Hemel Hempstead house, with its two cottages and five acres, but then Great White End was undoubtedly a good buy at the price we paid for it.

In 1953, after two years as an Assistant Under Secretary I was again moved up, to be the Deputy Under Secretary of State for Administration, a post which carried the old title of Chief Clerk. There were in those days only three Deputy Under Secretaries—Political, Economic and Administration—so that at the age of forty-four I was, nominally at any rate, one of the four senior officials in the Office. My period in Personnel Department had qualified me to some extent for this new post, while as Private Secretary I had acquired a good deal of useful knowledge about the working of the Service as a whole.

I was lucky to inherit very good heads of the Departments which now came under me, including notably John Henniker★ as head of Personnel Department. As against this my task became more difficult as a result of the change in Permanent Under Secretaries which had taken place at the same time as my appointment, William Strang being succeeded by Ivone Kirkpatrick. Ivone had a first-class mind and could be a delightful companion, but he was intolerant and sometimes lacking in judgment in his handling of staff. There are one or two among the present senior members of the Service whom he wished to write off as useless and whom I

★ Sir John Henniker-Major, later Ambassador to Jordan and Denmark.

sought to defend with some degree of success. Instead of trying to stand up for members of the Service against public or political criticism he tended to assume without investigation that such criticism was justified. On financial and organisational matters he was always looking for the maximum economies, which up to a point was right and proper, but it meant that when I was trying to negotiate with the Treasury for improvements in financial conditions for the Service I was liable to find that my own Permanent Under Secretary had joined forces with the opposition. It was, in my view, fortunate that his successor was Derick Hoyer Millar,* a person of great good sense and sound judgment who did much to restore the slightly shaken morale of the Office. Meanwhile, in spite of frequent arguments and disagreements, my relations with Ivone Kirkpatrick remained quite amicable, and he cannot have had too low an opinion of my efforts or he would not have allowed my name to go forward for a KCMG, which I received in the New Year Honours list in 1956. This was of course partly in recognition of earlier services, notably as Private Secretary. I cannot pretend that it did not give me satisfaction.

During my period as Chief Clerk the Select Committee on Estimates carried out an investigation of Foreign Office expenditure. My assistants and I spent a lot of time preparing papers for the Committee, and I was frequently summoned to give evidence, all of which was recorded and ultimately published. I think we were unlucky in the composition of the Committee for they had embarked on their task with the preconceived ideas that the Foreign Service was overstaffed and overpaid, and they disregarded all evidence to the contrary. In due course they produced a report which was even more critical and prejudiced than I had anticipated, and which at first sight looked as though it might do the Foreign Office a good deal of harm. It soon became clear, however, that the report was full of mistakes and of statements which were in direct contradiction with the published evidence. It was therefore not difficult to produce a short paper effectively refuting many of the Committee's conclusions. We were able to obtain good publicity for the Foreign Office rejoinder, and in the end little damage was done. The experience did not enhance my opinion of our parliamentarians.

* Sir Frederick Hoyer Millar, now Lord Inchyra.

In January 1956 I collapsed while out pigeon shooting one evening, and was out of action for several weeks. I suppose that I had for some years been overworking. In any case the powers that be in the Foreign Office decided that I ought to have a change and be sent to a not too arduous post. A few months later I was appointed Ambassador to Copenhagen, whither we were to proceed in the early autumn. I had now been at the Foreign Office for more than twelve years on end, so we were certainly overdue for a posting abroad, and Copenhagen was in many ways a pleasant prospect. Our two eldest daughters, Gillian and Susan, then aged twenty-one and nineteen, were to accompany us, while Davina remained at a finishing school and our son, Joe, at his preparatory school.

The Copenhagen Embassy is a splendid eighteenth-century house, a 'Palais' as the Danes call it, rather noisy and not at all conveniently planned, but with fine rooms for entertaining. The Danes are, of course, notably Anglophile, and most hospitable, and life in Copenhagen was easy and agreeable. I had an awkward time soon after my arrival trying to explain and defend our policy over Suez. The Danes found our behaviour inexplicable and I was privately inclined to agree with them. (I shall elaborate slightly on this in a later chapter.) After that, apart from occasional arguments about trade or fishery questions, there was little to disturb Anglo-Danish relations. At the same time their very closeness involved me in a great deal of speech-making and other representational activities. We were helped by having a highly successful State Visit to Denmark in May 1957 (of which also I shall have more to say later) and we had a regular flow of British Ministers and other distinguished visitors, including, on two occasions, Field Marshal Montgomery, coming to stay. Monty greatly surprised an audience of sceptical Danes by telling them that in his view the next great war would be fought between Russia and China. Ten years later the idea of such a clash seemed by no means so far-fetched.

Embassy functions in Copenhagen were enlivened by the presence of our daughters, who helped to lighten otherwise possibly staid dinner parties and who attracted many young Danes to the house. When, after a year or so the two elder girls decided to return to jobs in London, a Danish newspaper announced with

c

evident satisfaction that the British Ambassador 'had a daughter in reserve', and Davina come out to join us, and proved no less of a success with the Danes than her sisters. Embassies can be rather austere and un-homelike, and are greatly helped by the presence of children—and, I would add, dogs. Incidentally, none of the three girls married Danes, which was perhaps surprising. Susan and Gillian were both married in London in the course of 1959 and Davina was married from home three years later. We have been very fortunate in our three sons-in-law.

It soon became known to our Danish friends that I was a keen shot and on the strength of this we were invited to stay in many delightful Danish country houses. These visits provided opportunities to meet people whose outlook on current problems was often quite different from that of the citizens of Copenhagen. I also welcomed the chance to learn more about Danish agriculture and forestry, both very efficient and well-organised and key factors in the national economy (though perhaps slightly less so now than they were then).

One notable adventure during our time in Denmark was an official visit, at the invitation of the Danish Government, to the Faroes and Greenland. Having tentatively consulted the Admiralty about the possibility of going in one of HM ships, I was surprised and delighted to learn that if we could fit in with their dates, a cruiser, HMS *Bermuda*, could be made available. There was a slight problem about providing accommodation for Jean, particularly as there was also going to be an Admiral, Sir Royston Wright, on board, but it was finally agreed that I should embark at Rosyth and undertake the visit to the Faroes en route, and that she should fly out to join us at the Greenland capital, Godthaab. There she came to live on board (there being really no reasonable alternative) and for the next ten days we had a fascinating time paying visits to various small settlements along the south-west coast of Greenland, and penetrating as far north as the ice conditions would allow, which meant to Disko Bay. No ship of the size of the *Bermuda* had ever been seen before in places like Godthaab, and I do not think such a venture is ever likely to be repeated. For one thing cruisers are now almost an extinct species, and for another I do not believe that the Admiralty had appreciated what a hazardous undertaking it was for a ship like *Bermuda*, which had not been specially designed for those waters. However, in spite of inadequate charts and the constant risk of damage to the propellers from floating ice, all went well, and we were able to complete our programme more or less according to plan.

The Greenland scenery was magnificent, and particularly when the sun shone the pale greens and blues of the ice against the dark blue of the water made a dazzling spectacle. One morning my wife asked the steward who called her what it looked like outside, and received the answer, 'Icebergs, m'Lady. Icebergs as big as Marble Arch.' In reality they were often far larger. One evening we had some gunnery practice, the target being an iceberg at a range of about two miles. Our six-inch shells made practically no impression and a torpedo had equally little effect. The average berg is of incredible toughness and solidity, and judging by what was visible above the surface this whole berg must have weighed many thousands of tons. The only drawback on the whole expedition was the mosquitoes, which were very large and very hungry, and seriously reduced the pleasure of some of our trips ashore. If tourism in Greenland is ever to be developed—and there are great possibilities—something will have to be done to reduce their number or keep them at bay.

Roy Wright and I had hoped to have some good fishing—for Arctic Char, which resemble small salmon—but unfortunately it was an unusually late season and we had little success, though the locals were catching them with a species of gaff in the sea pools.

Eventually the cruiser had to leave us in order to participate in tercentenary celebrations at Bermuda, and we transferred to a small Danish coaster, the *Julius Thomsen*. Like other vessels which ply in those waters she was painted scarlet to make her conspicuous if stuck in the ice, and being specially designed for these conditions was able to grind her way through quite thick icepacks. We did not live in quite such state as on *Bermuda* (where we never failed to put on a black tie for dinner) but were nevertheless entertained most hospitably. Finally, from Julianahaab in the extreme south we flew back to Sondrestromfiord and thence to Copenhagen. Taking off in a small seaplane from a fjord full of blocks of floating ice had proved quite a hazardous undertaking, and we made three false starts before finally being airborne.

When I had been a little more than three years in Copenhagen the Foreign Office told me that my next post was to be that of Ambassador at The Hague. Before I had had time to get used to this idea, however, there was a change of plan and I was informed that I was wanted to come back to a new post of Deputy Under Secretary of State at the Foreign Office to handle relations with EFTA and the EEC—with the title of 'Adviser on European Trade Questions'. They wanted someone who would be likely to have the confidence of the Scandinavian Governments, and thought that I should fill the bill. I was quite attracted by the idea and of course it meant that we should be returning home to Great White End—though for me a good deal of travelling would be necessary.

We left Copenhagen in April 1960 and I started on my new duties almost at once. I found that the problem of our relations with the EEC was under re-examination in Whitehall and before very long we were moving towards a decision to apply for full membership. At the time I had a good many reservations about this, not least on account of our commitments to our EFTA partners.

The periodic EFTA ministerial meetings, which took me to all the other six capitals, as well as on numerous trips to what became the EFTA headquarters at Geneva, were cheerful and enjoyable occasions. Though from time to time there were sharp conflicts of interest, the EFTA atmosphere was always more relaxed and friendly than that which I was to encounter later in the EEC. (Incidentally I could never quite make up my mind whether to reveal to my EFTA friends that my charming spaniel had been christened Efta as a compliment to their association.)

I now found myself working closely first with Reggie Maudling, the President of the Board of Trade, and then, increasingly, with Ted Heath, who had been appointed Lord Privy Seal and established in the Foreign Office with special responsibility for European questions. After a few months my EFTA activities were supplemented by missions, which I had to lead, to the capitals of the six EEC countries to endeavour to ascertain how great were the problems which lay in the way of British membership, and to discuss possible solutions. These on the whole went well, with the exception of our talks with the French, who remained enigmatic, partly no doubt because the General had not yet made up his mind how to deal with the new situation created by the change in British policy.

When in due course the decision was taken to apply for membership I assumed that I should have some part in the negotiations. At one point this seemed to be in doubt and I was asked whether I would like to go as Ambassador to Athens. I asked to be excused, partly because having become involved in all the preliminary discussions I was reluctant to leave the Common Market field at that stage, and partly also because Jean and I had no wish to be uprooted again only a year or so after our return from Copenhagen.

The final composition of our negotiating delegation under Ted Heath was unexpected in that Bob Dixon,* our Ambassador in Paris, was asked to take on the job of official leader with Eric Roll† as his deputy. In addition there were senior representatives from the Commonwealth Relations Office, Board of Trade, Colonial Office, Ministry of Agriculture and Treasury, with myself from the Foreign Office. We came to be known as the 'Flying Knights', and Harold Macmillan has commented that 'never before in our history had we mustered so powerful and intelligent a number of men to serve so great an enterprise'. This may be over complimentary but I think it is in any case fair to say that we were a more high-powered team than any of those fielded by the existing member countries. One disadvantage of this was that none of us really had enough individual responsibility. Moreover, to expect Bob Dixon to combine the leadership of the Delegation with his duties as Ambassador in Paris was quite unreasonable.

Once the negotiations got under way we normally spent three or four days a week in Brussels, returning to London for briefing meetings on Saturdays and Mondays, and sometimes on Sunday. The negotiations, which were to last for some fifteen months, were an interesting and educative experience, but the constant travel and the erratic programme of meetings made life difficult. Altogether I look back on this period as one of the less enjoyable parts of my Foreign Office career, partly on account of the disruption of one's private life, but also because I felt my own position was a slightly invidious one and I was conscious that this type of conference diplomacy was not my strong suit. We should doubtless all have felt very differently if our negotiations had

* The late Sir Pierson Dixon.
† Later Sir Eric, economist and banker.

ended in success, but the General's veto put an end to our hopes and the final mood was naturally one of frustration.

I did have one personal cause for satisfaction, which was that our relations with our partners in EFTA had emerged relatively unscathed. They had been one of my special responsibilities, and, at a time when some of my colleagues in the delegation and a good many people in Whitehall tended to regard our EFTA undertakings as a millstone round our necks, I had insisted, with some success, that we must do nothing to impair our good relations with the other countries of the Association. It was just as well that this view prevailed, for when the negotiations broke down we were very glad to be able to fall back on EFTA.

After some weeks devoted to preparing reports on the negotiations and suggestions for the future, some of which may possibly have been of use to our successors seven years later, it was clear that I was available for some new job. I was sounded very tentatively as to whether I would like to be considered for the post of Ambassador to the EEC, but replied that I had had enough of the Community for some time to come. This feeling did not however apply to Brussels or Belgium, and when a little later on I learned that I was being considered for the Brussels Embassy I was quite content. In due course the appointment went through and in July 1963 we set off once more for Brussels where we had begun our diplomatic life.

When I left Brussels in 1936 there had been eight foreign Ambassadors, the lesser Powers being represented by Ministers— or not at all. On my return the numbers of Ambassadors had multiplied by ten and during my stay the numbers continued to increase fairly rapidly. This depreciation of the diplomatic currency was regrettable but in reality I suppose that not more than a dozen of my colleagues had a serious job to do. The rest cut little ice with either the Belgian Government or the people and their principal occupation seemed to be attending each other's parties.

Once again I was accredited to a Government with whom our relations were extremely close and friendly. In some ways an Ambassador to a country with which we are on bad terms may have a more challenging task, but the closer the links the more consultation there is, and the risk of misunderstandings is certainly not eliminated. The public relations side of the job is also much heavier—and this was notably the case in Brussels. More-over, during our five and a half years' stay we had a series of major events, a State Visit by the Queen and the Duke of Edinburgh, a 'British Week', and the 150th anniversary of the Battle of Waterloo, the preparations for all of which were spread over a year or more. So, what with the presence of the EEC and the transfer of NATO from France to Belgium, not to mention periodic crises over what was then the Congo, there was enough to keep me well occupied.

We were also fortunate in having a beautiful Embassy of manageable size, and, for most of the time, excellent domestic staff, so that entertaining was made easy. We had a fairly constant stream of visitors, both official and family and friends. Yet an-other advantage from my point of view was that we were again in a country where there was very good shooting, and I used to receive many more invitations than I could accept. Partly on this account there were few corners of Belgium which we did not visit in the course of our stay.

Now that the daughters were all married and our son, Joe, at Harrow, and later at Oxford, we had no children regularly living with us, though we always managed to have a daughter or two (and sometimes Joe) for major events like the Waterloo Ball, the State Visit and British Week, at which they were always great assets. Joe and his friends also helped to bring life to the house. Having earlier bracketed dogs with children I would add that our two tricolour cockers were well-known not only in the shooting field, where their behaviour was apt to be a bit erratic at least by British standards, but also at Embassy parties where they sat beside us as we received the guests.

The Brussels Embassy is not normally in the highest category, but in 1966 I had the satisfaction of being promoted to be a Grade I Ambassador, so that in every way Brussels was a satisfactory culmination of my diplomatic career.

By the time I reached the retiring age of sixty we had been in Brussels for five and a half years, and I was conscious that it was time for a change. Some people seem to suppose that the life of an Ambassador and his wife is an endless round of gay and enter-taining parties. In a capital like Brussels the social life is indeed very active, and though it may include many occasions which are interesting and enjoyable—we found we usually liked best the parties we gave ourselves—there are a good many unavoidable obligations which as time goes on become an increasing burden. Equally the amenities which go with the job—and which are an essential part of it—the spacious house and the ample domestic staff, the Rolls and the chauffeur constantly in attendance, the endless good meals, all after a time begin to pall. We at any rate were very ready to contemplate returning to a simpler and more natural life at home. Accordingly, much as we had enjoyed our time in Belgium, when the day of departure came and the lengthy goodbyes were over, we were quite happy to be going back to Great White End.

Looking back on my diplomatic career I am bound to recognise that I was extremely fortunate in my postings. Though I sometimes regret that I was never sent to any of the more exotic capitals—I should, for example, have enjoyed a spell in say Ethiopia or Iran—from the point of view of the upbringing of a family we had been exceptionally favoured.

To complete the story I should add that on my retirement I was invited to join the Board of the French subsidiary of Barclays Bank of which I later became the Chairman, and this was followed by other banking and business appointments which have meant that I have now embarked on a second, rather different, but, given my family background, not inappropriate career. My son Joe joined Barclays Bank at the same time as I did, and now that I have rectified my earlier straying from the fold he has become the eighth in direct line of father to son to have spent at least part of his life in the service of the Bank.

On re-reading this chapter I am conscious that it may all sound a bit complacent—an ideally happy marriage, delightful children (and grandchildren), a satisfying career, and so on. Apart from the great misfortune of the death of my mother I have indeed in many ways been very favoured. Perhaps also I have a natural tendency to look on the brighter side of things, which, together with a calm and equable disposition—a heritage maybe from those solid Quaker ancestors—were possibly useful assets when it came to dealing with a fairly temperamental Foreign Secretary. Anyhow it is now quite time to begin to describe what it was like to be in constant contact with, and I think I may say, the friend and confidant of that exceptional man, Ernest Bevin.

2

PRIVATE SECRETARY TO
MR BEVIN

I BECAME Principal Private Secretary to Mr Bevin on 6 March 1949. The appointment of Private Secretary was then, and doubtless still is, a coveted one in the Foreign Office and I had been very surprised to find myself suddenly earmarked for this rôle. In my previous job as Head of the Personnel Department I had known that a new Private Secretary would soon be needed and I had put forward the names of three colleagues who seemed to me to have all the necessary qualities. The first of the three, Evelyn Shuckburgh,* was destined to be my immediate successor, while the second, Tony Rumbold,† in due course replaced him, so that my recommendations were ultimately vindicated, but the powers that be in the Foreign Office decided to set aside my suggestions and to advise Mr Bevin to take me instead.

I had had a few encounters with Mr Bevin before this, but they were hardly enough to give him much idea of my capabilities, so there was no question of his having chosen me. He had, however, learnt by experience to rely to a large extent on the advice of his senior officials on such appointments, and accepted that a Minister, whose knowledge of the available candidates was inevitably limited, was unwise to try to make his own selection. When the news was first broken to me I protested that there were many others better qualified than myself, but my objections were overruled and I was soon summoned to see Mr Bevin to talk about my prospective appointment. I told him of my doubts about my suitability, but he brushed these aside and said that he assumed that I would not have been recommended to him if I had not been reliable, industrious and loyal, and that being so he was sure that

* Later Sir Evelyn, Ambassador to NATO and then to Italy.
† Sir Anthony Rumbold, Bart., later Ambassador to Thailand and to Austria.

the partnership would be a success; if it were not, he would con-sider it to be his fault. Somewhat reassured, I set to work to find out a little more about what the job involved.

Mr Bevin had had two other Principal Private Secretaries during the three and a half years that he had spent at the Foreign Office. The first had been Bob Dixon, whom he inherited from Anthony Eden. Bob had been a great success during his two years as Private Secretary to Eden and had been just as highly esteemed by Ernie Bevin. He had all the qualifications for this particular post, and indeed he was in every way an outstanding person, com-bining great charm of manner with exceptional intellectual gifts. He was just the man to help induct Mr Bevin at the Foreign Office, and he did a great deal to smooth the way for him during his early days there.

Bob Dixon remained with Mr Bevin for more than two years before being appointed Ambassador at Prague. The rest of his diplomatic career was equally distinguished and as already men-tioned he ended up as Ambassador in Paris. It was a tragedy that he died suddenly so soon after his retirement.

Bob Dixon's successor and my immediate predecessor was Frank Roberts, a friend of mine from Cambridge days (though some two years senior to me) and a man of many talents. He was later to be Ambassador in Moscow and finally a very active and effective Ambassador in Bonn. Mr Bevin had a great regard for Frank's ability and liked him personally, but Frank was possibly too dynamic a character to fit altogether easily into the rôle of Private Secretary. In any case Mr Bevin had decided at the end of 1948 that he would like to strengthen the High Commission at Delhi by sending Frank there as Deputy High Commissioner. Hence my opportunity.

I received plenty of good advice about what I would be required to do in my new post. The King's Private Secretary, Sir Alan Lascelles, was one of the first to impress on me that my most important duty was to ensure that my new master did not work himself to death, since it was in the country's interest that he should carry on as Foreign Secretary for as long as possible. I was given almost identical advice by the Chief of the Imperial General Staff,* and soon found that this was the view of many other impor-

* Field-Marshal Sir William (later Lord) Slim.

tant people, including our own newly appointed Permanent Under Secretary, William Strang.*

I also sought and obtained much valuable guidance from my two predecessors. Bob Dixon impressed on me that the essential function of the Private Secretary was to act as the link between the rest of the Foreign Office and the Secretary of State, to interpret the one to the other where necessary and to be constantly on the lookout to make sure that there was no friction. There had in the past been some Private Secretaries—and Oliver Harvey's *Diaries*† have since confirmed that he was most certainly one of them—who had tended to substitute their own views and recommendations for those of the departmental experts and who had gone to considerable lengths to force their ideas on the Secretary of State of the day. This, by the way, is how the Chef de Cabinet of a French, or for that matter, Belgian, Foreign Minister often operates. These officials usually exercise a strong personal influence over their Minister and enjoy a wide measure of independence within the Ministry—to the frustration of other departmental officers. Since the war, at any rate, this concept of the powers and functions of the Private Secretary has been frowned on in the Foreign Office, and I am sure that, as a result, the machine works more smoothly and harmoniously.

I do not mean to suggest that the Private Secretary should have no views or ideas of his own or that he should have no influence on his chief. Indeed, once he is accepted as a confidant he is bound to exercise considerable influence. But I maintain that he should be extremely careful not to take undue advantage of his privileged position, and he must be prepared sometimes to be self-effacing.

Incidentally, when my appointment was announced, a Hungarian newspaper, reading more into my name than was justified, published a cartoon headed 'A new Secretary—an obliging Principal', in which Mr Bevin was depicted as saying to me as I reclined in an armchair with one foot on his desk, 'Look here, Mr Barclay, I know very well what I owe to the son of a financial magnate. So when I ring it means that I beg you to be good enough to receive me in a few minutes.'

* Sir William Strang, later Lord Strang.
† *The Diplomatic Diaries of Oliver Harvey 1937–40* (London 1970). Ambassador to France 1948–54. Created Lord Harvey of Tasburgh.

I inherited a first-class team of assistants. My Number Two was Edward Tomkins, now Ambassador in Paris, always a stimulating and welcome companion, whose comments and advice were consistently helpful. Then came Christopher McAlpine (who has since left the Service), to be replaced before very long by Michael Wilford, now a Deputy Under Secretary of State in the Foreign Office. Each of these was a very efficient and quick worker, as indeed they had to be. The fourth occupant of our room was Pat Kinna, who was not a member of the senior branch of the Service but who had been with Mr Bevin longer than any of the rest of us and went with him when he finally left the Foreign Office to become Lord Privy Seal. Pat did sterling work looking after social engagements, travel plans, and, in particular, Mrs Bevin.* To support us we had a team of five girls, all highly competent and endlessly obliging, ruled over by a diminutive redhead, Alison David. They often worked very late at night but there was the compensation of periodic trips abroad which seemed to make up for a hard life in London—though for them the trips were scarcely rest-cures.

If any one member of the Private Office had been uncooperative or inefficient life would have been very difficult. Fortunately, in spite of the pressure under which we often worked, the atmosphere was always cheerful and good-humoured, and though I would not claim that we never made mistakes I think that the machine worked smoothly and well. This happy state of affairs was maintained when in due course Eddie Tomkins was replaced by Freddie Leishman.

To try to describe the main features of Mr Bevin's foreign policy would mean going well beyond the scope of this work, and is anyhow a task for the professional historians. Nevertheless, in order to understand the problems facing us when I came to work with him it is necessary to look back very briefly at what had happened since he took over as Foreign Secretary in July 1945.

I suppose it is true to say that the problem which then, and for many years to come, dominated all others was how to deal with the Russians, who had already proved such exceedingly awkward allies and who now held a dominant position in world affairs. There is little doubt that at the outset Mr Bevin hoped that some

* She was made Dame Florence after the death of her husband.

degree of cooperation with them might be possible, though he was far from sharing the rosy illusions of President Roosevelt and some of his advisers. These hopes were speedily dimmed by the Russian behaviour at the various post-war meetings and notably in the series known as the 'Conference of Foreign Ministers', which had been established by the Big Three at Potsdam and in which the Americans, French, Russians and ourselves participated. Russian actions in Germany and their refusal to cooperate with the other Occupying Powers were clearly discouraging, but it is probable that what finally convinced Mr Bevin that all hope of working together must be abandoned, at least for the time being, was the attitude of the Russians to the Marshall Plan Conference in 1947 and their attempt to frustrate the whole operation. It was now clear that their aim was to encourage disorder and prevent recovery in the countries of Western Europe.

The analysis of Russian policy in Winston Churchill's famous 'Iron Curtain' speech at Fulton, Missouri, in March 1946 had come as a shock to world opinion, but it is very likely that by then Mr Bevin was already inclined to agree with Churchill's rather gloomy assessment. His subsequent actions showed that he accepted that Western Europe was seriously threatened by Russia's aggressive policies. The Communist coup in Czechoslovakia and finally the Berlin blockade seemed to confirm his interpretation of Russian intentions.

Mr Bevin was deeply conscious of the military and economic weakness of the countries of Western Europe, including Britain, and set out to do what was possible to remedy the situation by creating a firm base for resisting Russian expansionism. The first step had been the Anglo-French Treaty of Dunkirk of March 1946, which had soon been followed by the Five Power Treaty of Brussels. At the outset, admittedly, the ostensible aim had been to prevent any revival of German aggressive tendencies, but the emphasis soon changed.

It was clear that Britain, France and the Benelux Powers were not in themselves strong enough to provide much of a barrier against Russian aggression in the West, and Mr Bevin began to work for a wider basis for Western collaboration which would bring in North America as well as some of the countries of Scandinavia and of Southern Europe. The assumption by the United

States of responsibility for economic and military assistance to Greece and Turkey by the Truman Declaration of March 1947 had been a very welcome step in the direction of transferring to the Americans a share of the burden of defence, which, as Mr Bevin had clearly perceived, had become too heavy for the United Kingdom. But this in itself did not go far enough, and in the course of 1948 negotiations began for what was to be known as the Atlantic Pact. Simultaneously, a movement towards greater co-operation among the countries of Western Europe was leading up to the establishment of the Council of Europe. Both sets of negotiations had reached their final stages when I became Private Secretary.

Meanwhile, on the economic front a great step forward had been taken towards the restoration of the shattered economies of the countries of Western Europe. It is generally accepted that one of Mr Bevin's great acts of statesmanship was his grasping of the opportunity offered by General Marshall's famous speech at Harvard in June 1947. He subsequently likened this to a life-line thrown to a sinking man, which, he said, 'we grabbed with both hands.' The immediate lead which he then gave resulted in the setting up of the Organisation for European Economic Cooperation. Though the countries of the Eastern bloc had opted out, this inaugurated a period of effective inter-governmental cooperation in the economic and financial fields which contributed largely to the rehabilitation of Western Europe.

The situation when I became Private Secretary was accordingly one of marked progress towards increasing cooperation among the Western Powers in both the political and the economic spheres. We were, however, confronted with many urgent and thorny problems. The Berlin blockade and the massive airlift which had been improvised to meet it were a source of constant anxiety and tension, and a serious incident, which could so easily have occurred, might have had disastrous consequences. The whole future of Germany was a complex problem which was to take up a great deal of our time in the next two years. Other pressing issues included the future of the ex-Italian colonies—Libya and Eritrea—Indonesia, Kashmir, relations with Egypt and the Arab world as a whole, and the emergence of Communist China.

Mr Bevin's Palestine and Middle Eastern policy is a large

subject in itself, and a good deal has already been written about it. It is often argued that Palestine was one of his notable failures, and it is certainly true that he did not attain his original objectives. To a large extent, however, he was the victim of forces outside his control. Priority had to be given to dealing with the aggressive policies of the Russians in Germany and elsewhere; the British people were exhausted and anxious to see the country's overseas liabilities reduced rather than extended; and at many points Mr Bevin found himself frustrated as a result of American internal policies. All this, however, belonged to the period before I came on the scene.

The problem now was to establish our relations with the new state of Israel on a satisfactory basis and to do so without weakening our system of military bases in Egypt and other Arab countries. Generally speaking Mr Bevin accepted the views of our defence chiefs on the need to maintain our military presence in the area but this meant that he had to appear in a rôle which he much disliked—that of preserver of the *status quo* and defender of the position of Arab kings and of 'the Pashas'. This troubled him considerably for his sympathies were with the common people of these countries rather than with their generally inefficient and reactionary Governments.

As I shall recount later on, a considerable proportion of our time during my first year as Private Secretary was spent at various international conferences, and on sundry trips outside Britain, and the demands on the Private Secretary when we were abroad were very different from those at home. First, however, I must try to give some idea of life in the Private Office when in London.

Mr Bevin was the first Foreign Secretary to occupy the ministerial flat on the second floor of No. 1 Carlton Gardens. This had been pleasantly furnished and equipped by the Ministry of Works and was of course conveniently close to the Foreign Office. It was very useful for informal meetings with British or foreign colleagues out of normal office hours and I got to know it pretty well during the next two years. The ground floor and first floor of the house were available for luncheon and dinner parties or receptions, and these too became very familiar. The flat was to be the Bevins' home until after his death, for Herbert Morrison never wanted to occupy it, preferring to stay on at No. 11 Downing Street—except at weekends, or sometimes in the week, when he returned to his own house at Eltham. Queen Mary, who was a warm admirer of Ernie Bevin, had given him a key to the adjoining garden of Marlborough House, but I do not think he often used it.

Mr Bevin normally began his day's work at between 4 and 5 a.m. and reckoned to spend three hours or more on his papers before breakfast. He preferred working in the early morning to the alternative of toiling on late at night, and since he normally woke up early he profited by this period, free from disturbance and interruption, not only to deal with his papers but also to ponder on the problems of the moment. I believe that this was a great source of strength.

There was invariably a mass of papers requiring the urgent attention of the Secretary of State, and every evening a messenger from the Foreign Office would take over to No. 1 Carlton Gardens a black box containing the latest telegrams and all the papers he needed for the work of the coming day—briefs for meetings of the Cabinet or the Foreign Policy Committee, for interviews with foreign Ambassadors or other visitors, drafts of speeches or answers to parliamentary questions and correspondence of every kind. Unless Mr Bevin was unwell he had usually got through all, or at least the greater part, of the contents of the box by breakfast time, and it would then be sent round to the Foreign Office in advance of his arrival.

My first job on getting to the office was to go through the box to see which papers had been disposed of and which required further discussion or consultation. A large E.B. at the bottom of a paper meant that it was approved. He seldom wrote much on any paper but there was sometimes a pithy comment, or more probably a scarcely legible scrawl indicating doubt or disagreement. Mr Bevin had left school at the age of eleven, and, though quite a quick reader, writing was still a rather laborious business. He had an enormous silver fountain pen—christened by Roger Makins* 'The Caber'—which he held between his first and second fingers. It had for long been the accepted practice for the Foreign Secretary to use red ink but he always stuck to blue-black. On

---

* Sir Roger Makins, then a Deputy Under Secretary of State in the Foreign Office, later Ambassador to the United States, Joint Permanent Secretary of the Treasury, etc. Created Lord Sherfield.

the various formal documents which required his signature he would write 'Ernest Bevin', sloping steeply upwards but in a clear hand. Otherwise the scrawls were often barely legible. I and my assistants became reasonably good at interpreting them, and we often used to write a translation underneath for the guidance of those who had to take action on the papers. The only person I have met whose writing was even more difficult to decipher was Hector McNeil, then Minister of State at the Foreign Office. If Ernie and he had tried to correspond direct the result would have been utter confusion.

By the time the Secretary of State appeared in his office, normally at about 10 a.m., I would be ready with one or two enquiries about the significance of some comment or the reasons for his dissent from some recommendation. Having heard what was troubling him I could sometimes resolve the difficulty, or if not I could elucidate his views or interpret his instructions for the benefit of those directly concerned. There would also, by the time of his arrival, be a mass of new telegrams or other papers needing his attention.

The Foreign Secretary's office is a large, very high, ornate room with windows looking on to the Horse Guards Parade and St James's Park, with much red leather and highly polished tables. There was one paticularly hard and uncomfortable sofa, on which Ernie used occasionally to curl up for a post-lunch nap. In those days the principal picture was a large portrait of George III, though why he should have been thus honoured I never discovered. Ernie Bevin was liable to point him out to any visiting American, saying, 'You see, 'e's my 'ero', and if necessary he would go on to explain how grateful he was to those whose policies had led to American Independence. I believe that George Brown had him replaced by Palmerston.

The Private Secretaries worked in an equally high and only slightly less ornate Victorian office, adorned with signed photographs of former Foreign Secretaries and with a connecting swing door to the Secretary of State's room. We also had a fine view on to St James's Park and looked down on the haunt of the pelicans. Occasionally, in winter I would see duck flighting past our window and sometimes wished that I could be translated to some East Anglian marsh.

D

When the Secretary of State was present our room was normally chaotic, with several telephones ringing, messengers coming in and out with red boxes and officials hurrying in with papers requiring urgent action or perhaps gathering for an office meeting with the Secretary of State. It was very difficult to dictate anything other than a brief note, or indeed to concentrate for any length of time, for one was constantly interrupted.

A good deal of the Secretary of State's time was spent in office meetings at which the Permanent Under Secretary, or some other senior official together with the experts primarily concerned, would come to explain some problem on which his views were required, or to seek guidance on how to reply to some urgent telegram. As Dean Acheson has written of Ernie, 'He could lead and learn at the same time', and when the officials had had their say and the Secretary of State had asked some probing questions he would give his reactions and indicate the general line he thought we should follow. This he would do in colourful but often slightly obscure language. It would then be for those concerned to go away and draft the necessary instructions for posts abroad or, it might be, prepare a paper for the Cabinet. These meetings often appeared rambling and rather chaotic and the conclusions reached were by no means always crystal clear, but the senior members of the Foreign Office had learnt to know the way the Secretary of State's mind worked and many of them were remarkably adept at producing with great speed a document which correctly represented his ideas. I normally sat in at all these conferences and was responsible for clearing the subsequent papers with him. The only meetings in his room which I did not usually attend were private talks with Cabinet colleagues or with the Permanent Under Secretary, and even then I was quite often asked to come in and join them.

A meeting of the Cabinet or of some other ministerial committee was usually preceded by last-minute discussions by the Secretary of State with the officials concerned with any Foreign Office items on the agenda. He also had to be shown any fresh telegrams which might affect the issue. He greatly disliked finding that one of his Cabinet colleagues had already seen a Foreign Office telegram which he had not yet had time to read, and this had to be avoided at all costs. I often used to go down with him in the lift or walk across to No. 10 Downing Street in order to impart some last-minute piece of information. Incidentally, I question whether Foreign Office items now occupy quite such a large proportion of the Cabinet's time as they did in that very disturbed period.

The Secretary of State seldom failed to return to his office when the Cabinet was over, even though this might mean that he would be late for a luncheon engagement, and he would then give me an advance report on how Foreign Office questions had fared. Where urgent action was required this made it possible to mobilise the officials concerned to begin the drafting of any necessary telegrams of instructions to posts abroad. If the Secretary of State was in no particular hurry I would probably be given a more detailed account of the proceedings, with fairly sharp and frank comments on some of his colleagues. He was often irritated by their failure to grasp the full significance of some Foreign Office problem which had been under discussion, and he sometimes complained to me with disgust that 'None of them seemed interested'. Stafford Cripps was by no means always on the same side as Ernie Bevin, but at least he earned credit for his critical and intelligent interest in foreign affairs, and the same was true of Nye Bevan, even though he too was often one of Ernie's principal antagonists. Advice or suggestions from the more junior Ministers were seldom welcomed and a fairly frequent comment was, 'That young man, 'e worries me.' Mr Attlee was of course Mr Bevin's principal confidant, and he could almost always be relied on to support him in any ministerial discussion. Partly for this reason, but primarily of course owing to his own dominating position and personality, it was very rare indeed for Mr Bevin not to get his own way with his colleagues. In the circumstances it is perhaps hardly surprising that he always described the Government's foreign policy as 'my policy'. He would announce, '*I* intend to do this', or, more often perhaps, '*I* won't have it'. It was to him a very personal matter.

A Foreign Affairs debate in the House of Commons was always a major undertaking. The first point to establish was whether the Foreign Secretary was to speak first or to wind it up. In the former case he would normally have a complete text for his speech which would be the outcome of numerous discussions within the Office, various officials having been instructed to contribute passages on their particular problems. The result was naturally something of a patchwork, and it was never easy to coordinate such a speech or give it satisfactory form. From time to time Mr Bevin would seize on a draft passage and say, 'This is not me', and proceed to re-draft it in his own language. The re-draft would then be passed to me or one of my assistants with instructions to 'Put that into the King's English'—which was sometimes easier said than done. Almost invariably there was a fearful scramble at the last moment to ensure that the speech in final form was typed in time.

If, on the other hand, Mr Bevin was winding up, he would announce that he would speak 'ex tempor'—as he always called it. All the same, draft passages on some of the points raised in the debate would be required, and there would be hastily summoned meetings in his room in the House of Commons at which he would indicate what he had in mind. Again there would be frantic typing out of passages for his possible use, usually ending up, miraculously, with a minute or two to spare. In the event he quite often set aside these notes, and when he did so the result was usually more interesting to listen to, even if sentences remained unfinished and new ideas chased each other in apparent disorder.

Mr Bevin more than once advised me to get used to speaking 'ex tempor'. In support of this he used to quote the example of a Trade Union friend of his who was due to make his first major public speech and had prepared himself for the occasion by writing it all out on a series of cards. Unfortunately, while the chairman of the meeting was making a short speech introducing him, Ernie's friend, who was a keen bridge player, started nervously to shuffle the pack of cards in his hand. The result, when he stood up to speak, was, predictably, utter confusion.

Mr Bevin was never at his best when speaking in the House of Commons. He had of course come to Parliament late in life, after his appointment as Minister of Labour in May 1940, and he never quite seemed to get the feel of the House. He made very effective speeches elsewhere, not only on occasions such as the Trade Union Congress or at political meetings (where he adopted a more forceful if not pugnacious style of oratory) but also at international gatherings such as the United Nations Assembly. He was at his best, however, on more informal occasions and then he could be both eloquent and entertaining. Among the best speeches I heard him make was one on the general theme of Anglo-American relations at a farewell dinner party for Mr Lew Douglas on his retirement from the United States Embassy in London. He was nearly always a success with American audiences.

Mr Bevin could be relied on to deal effectively with hecklers or with supplementary questions in the House of Commons. Interruptions more often came from the back-benchers on his own side of the House and without turning his head round he would hurl some crushing retort over his shoulder at anyone who was daring to butt in or to criticise. He was also adept at dealing with the Press, though there were sometimes complaints that he had told them nothing new.

When Mr Bevin was speaking 'ex tempor' his meaning was usually quite clear to his listeners and the main thread of his argument was easily followed. When, however, his words were taken down textually the result could look very odd. He was the despair of our own shorthand typists, for when dictating he would pour forth a stream of words without apparent punctuation and with little regard for syntax or grammar. The only thing for them to do was to take it down verbatim and then I or one of the other Private Secretaries would endeavour to put it into proper shape. We had a problem with his speeches in the House for the Hansard reporters have strict rules forbidding the subsequent amendment of the substance of speeches or anything in the nature of editing. As soon as a speech was over I or one of my assistants used nevertheless to hurry up to their room and ask to see their draft record. Sometimes this made no sense at all. If, as frequently happened, they had been confused by Mr Bevin's idiosyncratic pronunciation we were able to elucidate, and we usually managed to persuade them to let us make the minimum amendments necessary to make the whole thing comprehensible to the reader, provided always that we did not seem to be changing the substance.

Like Sir Winston Churchill, Mr Bevin had his own way of pronouncing foreign names, and once he had adopted a certain pronunciation he would not change, even though everyone else might prefer a different rendering. Count Sforza, the Italian Foreign Minister (for whom he did not much care) was always known as 'that man Storzer'. Ecuador became 'Eucador', Senor Bramuglia was 'Bramgulia' and Guatemala was 'Gutemelia'.

There was a celebrated occasion when the Guatemalan Ambassador came to protest about some frontier incident with British Honduras (as it then was). Ernie listened to him for a while and then became irritated. 'Where was it you said you came from ?', he asked the surprised Ambassador, and when the latter said rather pompously that he was the Ambassador of Guatemala Ernie replied, 'Gutemelia, Gutemelia ? Why, I never 'eard of the place until this morning!' Quite untrue, of course, and not exactly rapier-like diplomacy but it effectively crushed the Ambassador, who withdrew as quickly as possible. Ernie Bevin was in reality remarkably well informed about Latin America, and one South American Ambassador in London commented with surprise that Ernie seemed to know more about his country than he did himself.

I remember another occasion when Ernie used somewhat similar sledgehammer tactics with a foreign Ambassador who had incurred his displeasure. It was in Paris and the victim was the Italian Ambassador who had come to convey some message from his Government about the ex-Italian colonies. Before he had got far Ernie interrupted him, saying, 'I know all abour your disgraceful behaviour during the war. You engaged in mischievous intrigues in Afghanistan. I am not going to listen to a lecture from someone like you.' The source of this information about the Ambassador's wartime behaviour in Afghanistan was definitely unquotable, but the accusation was not altogether without foundation. The Italian emerged from the interview severely shaken and observed as I saw him out that dealing with a Foreign Minister like Mr Bevin was indeed a novel experience.

I do not want to give the impression that Ernie Bevin was often truculent or aggressive in his treatment of foreign Ambassadors. As a general rule he treated them with every consideration, though he could be pretty outspoken with those he knew well, like Lew Douglas. Lew gave as good as he got and there were sometimes quite rough passages between them, but they remained very good friends.

As was only to be expected, Ernie Bevin was no linguist and he only knew a few words of French. This of course was no problem at conferences or other international occasions at which there were official interpreters. At private meetings with the French Foreign Minister, Monsieur Robert Schuman, who had a fair understanding of English but could not speak it, I often found myself having to interpret. It is naturally very much easier to interpret into one's own language than into another, and given a relatively slow speaker like Monsieur Schuman and subjects with which I was familiar I could manage well enough. Translating Mr Bevin into French was much more tricky, and this usually required a combined effort between Monsieur Schuman's Chef de Cabinet and myself. One of my more difficult assignments was when, after a small but festive dinner party at the Quai d'Orsay, Ernie turned to me and said, 'Now let's tell Monsieur Schuman my story about the bull in a bowler 'at.' This was a story which might have gone down well enough in an English pub, but translated into French in a salon of the Quai d'Orsay it was not a great success.

Mr Bevin studying a restaurant menu in French was always an entertainment. When I and one or two others were dining with him in the Penthouse of the Hotel Bristol in Paris in the autumn of 1949 he turned to me and said, 'Roddie, let's have some newts for dinner.' This, being interpreted, meant a bottle (or bottles) of Nuits St Georges. There were other occasions when astonished waiters were ordered to bring 'a bottle of newts', and a little explanation became necessary.

Going back to the question of proper names, I recall only one instance when Mr Bevin showed interest in the correct pronunciation of a name, that of Mr Senanayake, then Prime Minister of Ceylon, whose guest he was to be. I was a bit doubtful about it myself, but soon found out for him and he thereafter got it right. Incidentally, his pronunciation of English names was also sometimes unorthodox, and when we crossed the Atlantic on the same ship as Miss Deborah Kerr she was always referred to as Debōrah Curr.

During the first few weeks after my appointment I had a struggle to keep abreast with all that was going on, particularly as many of the subjects were new to me and I had to read up the back history. I made life more difficult for myself by living out of London—it took me about one hour and a quarter home to office, door to door—but my family was happily installed in the country and I could not afford to maintain two establishments. My solution was to spend two or more nights a week in the Foreign Office, where a small bedroom was available for me, and after dining at my club or elsewhere, I would go back and work till midnight or later, catching up on the unceasing flow of papers.

The Secretary of State tried to restrict the number of his social engagements, particularly at night, but from time to time he would dine at some foreign Embassy and there were other evening parties of an official nature which he could hardly avoid attending. He also had to act as host at a good many government luncheons or dinners for distinguished foreign visitors or for foreign Ambassadors who were leaving London. He was a very good host on such occasions and usually enjoyed himself, but the hours of work he put in on the contents of the box the following morning tended to vary inversely with the number of glasses of brandy he had consumed.

We tried to avoid making official engagements for the Secretary of State on Saturdays, but he always came into the office at his customary hour and normally stayed till 2 or 3 o'clock, foregoing lunch. Bob Dixon, in his *Diary*,* noted that as a result he too missed lunch—at least on the first Saturdays after Ernie Bevin's arrival at the Foreign Office, but being forewarned I generally arranged to have sandwiches at my desk. Since Ernie was not under the usual pressure, this was a good opportunity to talk over plans or get his views on problems that were looming ahead. With luck I would be home in time for tea.

The first weekend after I had taken over, the Secretary of State was going down to Chequers. I thought this sounded like a nice change for him but he was unenthusiastic. 'You don't get enough to eat, they give you sherry in glasses the size of thimbles and the only warm room in the house is the lavatory'—was his gloomy forecast. On Monday morning I enquired how he had fared and he replied that it was just as he had anticipated.

A few months later—at the end of August—I was bidden to accompany him to Chequers and was curious to see whether it was as austere as he made out. Apart from the Attlees and Ernie the party consisted of Cripps, Gaitskell, Harold Wilson and

* *Double Diploma. The Life of Sir Pierson Dixon*, by Piers Dixon (London, 1968).

Edward Bridges,* and the subject under discussion was the
imminent devaluation of the pound. I do not know quite why I was
there except that Ernie liked to have me with him. He and I
stayed for dinner, which was by no means as meagre as he had led
me to expect, before returning to London. When, in later years,
during the Common Market negotiations I stayed there once or
twice as one of Ted Heath's guests, I found that the lesser bed-
rooms were not the height of comfort but there was certainly no
hardship involved. The food and drink were good, and the rose
garden and the lawn, and indeed the whole atmosphere of the
place made a great impression on our foreign visitors.

As time went on I acquired fascinating glimpses into Ernie
Bevin's youth. On our first trip on the *Queen Mary* he told me as
we approached New York that I must be sure to tip the lift boy.
'You know, I was a pageboy once myself,' he said. I found it
difficult to picture him in a pageboy's uniform. On another
occasion I went into his room at the Foreign Office and heard him
saying on the telephone, 'You want to beat it and then put olive
oil on it.' He turned round with a grin and said, 'Mrs Bevin's got
a tough bit of steak and wants to know how to treat it. You know I
was once assistant to a chef in a restaurant in Bristol.' Incidentally
Mrs Bevin had no hesitation in ringing him up with domestic
queries of this kind, and always assumed that they should have
priority over affairs of state.

At one stage in his early career Ernie had worked for a Bristol
laundry. Here, he told us, he invented some special way of ironing
ostrich feathers on ladies' hats, and this earned him a bonus.
Later on he had driven a ginger-beer van and this he had turned
into a grandstand at the wedding of (I think) Clara Butt, charging
spectators a small sum for the privilege of standing on it. As a
result of his time as a van driver he knew quite a bit about horses
and when he came to spend a Sunday at our house near Hemel
Hempstead, our daughters' ponies were paraded for his inspection. He commented on them quite knowledgeably and from then
on whenever he saw Jean he would greet her with ''Ow are the
'orses ?' He was a strong supporter of blood sports and when there
was a debate in the House on some back-bencher's anti-hunting

* Sir Edward Bridges, Permanent Secretary of the Treasury. Later
created Lord Bridges.

bill he insisted on going, at some inconvenience, to record his vote against it. He told me that he had enjoyed following hounds on foot in his youth and anyhow he was opposed to legislating about people's pastimes. During the war he had opposed a proposal to ban horse racing for the duration, and had won his point.

If I had had a day's shooting (I had two rather lean seasons during my period as Private Secretary), I would sometimes take Ernie a brace of pheasants, and one Monday morning I mentioned that I had some birds for him and would give them to his driver. 'You give them to me, me boy,' he replied. 'I'm not too grand to carry me dinner 'ome.' On another occasion I took him a brace of pheasants as a present from my brother-in-law, John Gladstone. Ernie commented that this was not the first time that he had eaten Gladstone pheasants. He used to have a poacher friend who lived near Hawarden and who from time to time would get him a bird or two.

Ernie was always very ready to put on a morning coat, or for that matter a dinner jacket, but felt uncomfortable in a white tie and tails and avoided these whenever possible. He firmly refused to wear a top hat. He told me that he had only once in his life worn a top hat and that was when as a young man he substituted for one of his brothers driving a hearse.

From time to time Ernie would reminisce about his Trade Union days and I learnt of some of the pitfalls to be avoided when organising a strike. It was important, he told me, to avoid getting at odds with the police, and this meant that you had to keep a firm hand on the hotheads. On one occasion when they had had a strike at the docks at Avonmouth the strike committee headquarters had been some miles away in Bristol. There was one particular enthusiast who was spoiling for a fight, so Ernie arranged that he should act as messenger and told him that he would have the responsible job of carrying important communications to strike headquarters. There was no public transport and it was very hot, and the man arrived, exhausted but triumphant, and handed over his vital message, which, had he but known, merely said, 'We're trying to keep this B.F. out of mischief.'

I have so far kept off the subject of health, but this was in reality a crucial consideration in every plan we made. By the time

I took over as Private Secretary Ernie Bevin was quite a sick man. He had had an attack of coronary thrombosis in 1946 and though he had made a reasonably good recovery from this he was now subject to fairly frequent attacks of angina. These fortunately did not last very long but they were exhausting and painful and he much disliked people seeing him when one was in progress. Any physical exertion, and in particular walking upstairs, was liable to bring one on. When travelling abroad, therefore, one of the first things to ensure was that he would not be obliged to climb any long flights of stairs, and if there was no lift available where he was staying we tried to arrange that he should sleep on the ground floor. Walking up the gangway onto the *Queen Mary* on our first trip together across the Atlantic was enough to bring on an attack, and unfortunately there were pressmen and photographers present so that it did not pass unnoticed. We also had trouble when in May 1949 we went to Berlin to see the airlift in progress. A reception for him had been organised by the Berlin City authorities, no lifts were working and there was a long flight of stairs to be climbed. Half way up we stuck, and some tablets were thrust into Ernie's hand. After a slight delay he was able to resume his slow plod upstairs but it had been an awkward moment. One of us—it was usually Ernie's faithful detective, Ben Masey— always had available a spare box of these tablets—which Ernie called his 'pellets'—and they seemed to give immediate relief.

Flights by ordinary commercial aircraft were ruled out, and the only ones permitted were those by special plane when it could be guaranteed that we would not go above a height of, I think, 5,000 feet. This enabled us to fly into Berlin in a RAF York and back in the High Commissioner's private plane, and on another occasion we flew in a RAF aircraft from Rome to Malta and thence to Fayid on the Suez Canal. These low altitude flights were all right provided the weather was good, but we had a bumpy trip coming back from Berlin, and when flying over the Mediterranean on our way to Egypt the pilot suddenly announced that to avoid trouble we must climb to a height above our permitted ceiling. Fortunately on this occasion we had with us Mr Bevin's doctor, Sir Alec McCall, so that I was able to pass the responsibility for the decision on to him.

Alec McCall had been looking after Mr Bevin since 1943 and

was devoted to his undisciplined and unruly patient, though from time to time he would become exasperated and threaten to throw his hand in. On one occasion, in Moscow, he had got as far as packing his bags to return to London but the weather made flying impossible and to Ernie's satisfaction he was obliged to stay on. Fortunately Ernie had great confidence in him and liked to have him around. 'This is Alec,' he would say. ' 'E treats my be'ind like a dartboard.' This had become a favourite form of introduction, but I believe the first time he used the phrase was when he and George VI were comparing notes on what they suffered at the hands of their doctors.

Alec McCall was a great source of help and comfort to the Private Secretaries, and when he accompanied us on trips abroad, as he often did when an absence of more than a few days was involved, this greatly eased things for me. I could always turn to him for advice on any particular engagement or commitment and if I said that it was essential that the Secretary of State should appear at such and such a place at a given time Alec would always ensure by dint of an injection or a tablet that Mr Bevin was on parade and able to do whatever was required of him. If Alec was not there I had to use my own judgment as to what was possible, and from time to time would have to decide that some item must be struck off the programme if all the really essential engagements were to be kept. When in London Alec was less in evidence, but throughout this period he and I kept in very close touch and throughout 1950 Alec saw Ernie almost every day.

It was not only his heart—'the old ticker' as Ernie called it— that was giving trouble. Indeed, Alec told me that almost the only sound part of Ernie's body was his feet—and they had quite a heavy task, for he weighed 18 stone!

Until the last few months of his time as Foreign Secretary, and leaving out of account two periods in the spring and summer of 1950 when he was temporarily out of action as a result of operations for piles (the first of which was apparently bungled), Mr Bevin's normal working week would have been enough to exhaust a much younger and fitter man. This was only achieved as a result of sheer determination and at the cost of considerable physical suffering, but he remained passionately interested in the job and his grip on affairs never really weakened. He never took more than a fortnight's holiday a year (which incidentally meant that I could not take more either) and even then he was liable to be pursued by special messengers with boxes of papers. While in hospital after his operations he liked to be kept informed of all important developments, and I used to visit him regularly. He was very sensitive to any suggestions in the Press or by his political opponents (or, for that matter, members of his own Party) that he was no longer fit enough for the job. They tended to make him all the more determined to carry on, but he was sometimes assailed with doubts whether he would be able to do so much longer. He used periodically to ask me what I thought, and until he fell ill with pneumonia in the beginning of 1951 I had no hesitation in replying that I considered that from the point of view of the national interest the longer he could stay at the Foreign Office the better. I used sometimes to compare notes with William Strang, and we always came to the conclusion that Ernie Bevin, even if operating at something considerably less than full efficiency, was a more effective Foreign Secretary than any of the possible candidates for the succession was likely to be. Looking back on it I believe we were quite right.

In the autumn of 1950 the Prime Minister suggested to Mr Bevin that he should give up the Foreign Office and become Chancellor of the Exchequer, the idea being that this would spare him a lot of arduous travelling. When Mr Attlee was forming his Government after the Labour victory in 1945 his intention at one stage had been to appoint Mr Bevin to the Treasury, and this was what the latter had confidently expected, and indeed desired. There have been differing accounts of what caused Mr Attlee to change his plans at the last minute and to switch Dr Dalton to the Treasury and Mr Bevin to the Foreign Office, but it seems probable that the King's comment to him that the latter would be a good appointment had a good deal to do with it. The Bevins had been planning a short holiday in Devon after the turmoil of the election, and he used to enjoy telling how he rang up Mrs Bevin and told her, 'It's not Devonshire for me tomorrow, but Potsdam,' to which she characteristically replied, 'Potsdam, what on earth is that?'

It is interesting to speculate on what might have happened if Mr Bevin had gone to the Treasury in 1945. He had quite a good basic understanding of economic problems but though he would doubtless have made his mark as Chancellor I do not think for a moment that his remarkable gifts would have had as much scope there as at the Foreign Office. In any case, when Mr Attlee made his suggestion towards the end of 1950 it was much too late to make a change. Mr Bevin had by now acquired an intimate know- ledge of all the Foreign Office problems of the day, and though the load was very heavy he at least knew the background and the personalities involved, as well as the techniques of diplomacy. At the Treasury he would have been confronted with fresh and complicated problems and I think he probably realised that to master them would have called for an effort of which he was no longer capable. At any rate it was quite clear to me that though he might continue for a while at the Foreign Office he no longer had the resilience to tackle a new commitment of the magnitude of the Treasury. A further consideration for him was that he did not at all relish the idea of handing over the Foreign Office to one of his colleagues—for he did not think that any of them (with the possible exception of Hector McNeil, who was not considered senior enough) was qualified to take on such a responsibility.

Very few people knew about the Attlee suggestion and I do not know who else Mr Bevin consulted before replying, but when he asked me what I thought I had no hesitation in advising him, for the reasons given above, to turn down the well-meant offer. He was relieved to find that I entirely agreed that he should decline and ask to be allowed to remain where he was, and this he duly did.

When, a few months later, Mr Bevin went down with pneu- monia, I was forced to accept that he was unlikely to be able to carry on much longer. Though he made a reasonably good recovery he had clearly aged a good deal, and as he was approaching his seventieth birthday this was hardly surprising.

It had been agreed, in view of the affection and esteem in which he was held throughout the Foreign Service, that we should join together to give him a seventieth birthday present, and though the suggested contribution was (if I remember right) only two shillings we had no difficulty in collecting a considerable sum of money. He told me that he and Mrs Bevin wanted a dinner service and that he himself would like a kneehole desk for his retirement.

In that period of continuing shortages it was not easy to get hold of a good new dinner service but this was finally achieved and I also found him a handsome desk. A small birthday party was arranged at the Foreign Office at which a token plate and the desk were to be handed over, and this would normally have been a very cheerful occasion. Unfortunately, the Prime Minister had that very day told the Secretary of State that he thought it was time for him to give up. Though Ernie must have realised that this was now almost inevitable he would have liked to take the decision himself, and his first reaction was one of resentment. The speed with which Mr Attlee wished to act was a further grievance, and what made matters even worse was that his successor was to be the much disliked Herbert Morrison. Altogether his last few days at the Foreign Office were an unhappy time. As I saw him off for the last time from the Park Door he looked old and frail and miserable. There was nothing I could say which could offer much comfort. Anyhow I was feeling a bit emotional myself.

Ernie Bevin was to remain in the Cabinet as Lord Privy Seal, but in fact his departure from the Foreign Office was virtually the end of his career, and only five weeks later, on 14 April 1951, the 'old ticker' finally gave out. I went to see him at his flat, where he was in bed with a heavy cold, the day before he died, and found him in good spirits and keen to have news of various friends. The end came suddenly, while Mrs Bevin was out at a football match. But here I am jumping ahead, and I must now give some account of the very different life led by both the Foreign Secretary and his Private Secretary when on trips abroad.

3

TRAVELS WITH MR BEVIN

OF MY FIRST YEAR as Private Secretary nearly six months were spent out of the country. We were, of course, still in the period of conferences concerned with the post-war settlements, which inevitably involved the Foreign Ministers of the principal Allied Powers. Moreover our absences tended to be prolonged by the limitations imposed on the Secretary of State's travel by air. He was not allowed to fly across the Atlantic so we always went on one of the *Queens*—or on the *Mauretania*—and when we later went to Colombo we again travelled nearly all the way there and back by sea.

Wherever Mr Bevin went I went too. I soon realised that he liked to have me always in attendance and I found also that for the sake of continuity it was very desirable, if not positively essential, to accompany him on all his trips abroad. One of the other Private Secretaries usually came too, as well as two of our lady secretaries and one, or sometimes two, detectives.

In many ways the responsibilities of the Private Secretary were greater and more varied when we were away from London. If a new crisis blew up when we were at home all the experts were on the spot to give advice and undertake all the necessary paper work. If, however, we were say in Washington, and had gone there primarily to discuss the future of Germany, we would obviously have with us the chief European experts but possibly no others. If fresh trouble arose in the Middle East or perhaps South-East Asia and the Secretary of State was asked by the Cabinet or the Foreign Office to give his views or to issue directives, he would naturally look to the Private Secretaries for supplementary information or advice. It was accordingly essential to have an adequate background knowledge of all the current issues and potential troublespots.

I did not have long to wait before my first trip abroad, for less than three weeks after my arrival I found myself setting off with the Secretary of State to Washington, primarily for the signing of the Atlantic Pact (the name which was then commonly used for the North Atlantic Treaty), but also for tripartite discussions with the Americans and the French on German problems. Final agreement on the text of the Pact had been reached in the week after I took over, and the Secretary of State had made a statement about it in the House of Commons and had also broadcast to the nation, explaining its purpose and scope. He had not wanted to have a debate in the House until after the Pact had been signed, but much to his annoyance Herbert Morrison (then leader of the House) agreed with the Opposition that one should take place immediately before our departure. This was certainly inconvenient but the debate provided an occasion for the Secretary of State to receive many bouquets, from the Opposition as well as from his own Party, so in the end he was mollified. He had earlier received a message of congratulations from the King which gave him much satisfaction. The final success of the negotiations, and indeed the whole concept of the Treaty, had undoubtedly owed much to Mr Bevin himself, and he was very naturally elated by the outcome. He would have liked the signature ceremony to have taken place in Bermuda, but there was opposition to this from the Americans and others, and he had to agree reluctantly that it should be in Washington. This was certainly a more practical arrangement, the more so in view of the other matters requiring discussions with the State Department.

When planning a trip abroad two of the questions that arose were, first—was Mrs Bevin coming too, and secondly—were we going to stay at the Embassy or at a hotel? On this occasion it was decided that Mrs Bevin should not accompany us and that we were to stay at the Embassy, though there had been a moment when this had been in doubt. It so happened that Sir Winston Churchill was then in the United States and it seemed that we might overlap with him in Washington where he was due to stay with the Ambassador, Oliver Franks.* This caused an explosion from Ernie, who said that he was not prepared to stay at the Embassy if he had to play second fiddle. In the end all was well

* Sir Oliver, later Lord Franks. Subsequently Chairman of Lloyds Bank, Provost of Worcester, etc.

E

as the dates did not clash. Accordingly on this occasion and indeed on all our future visits to Washington we stayed, very comfortably, with the Franks. I of course already knew the house well from my wartime service in Washington, though I had not previously stayed there.

There was the usual frantic rush before our departure from the Foreign Office, and I remember the feeling of relief when we were finally ensconced in the boat train at Waterloo, complete with half a dozen of the red leather despatch boxes containing official documents which invariably accompanied the Secretary of State on trips abroad (in distinction to the black boxes which we used in London). There was a crowd of reporters, photographers and others to see us off. As our train drew slowly into the station at Southampton a group of dockers and railwaymen standing beside the track spotted the Secretary of State at the window and shouted out, 'Good old Ernie!'—much to his gratification. As already mentioned, our arrival on board the Queen Mary was complicated by Ernie having a heart attack going up the gangway, but on reaching his cabin he recovered quite quickly, and a glass of champagne all round had a beneficial effect.

These periodic journeys by sea undoubtedly did the Secretary of State a lot of good. The days before our departure were invariably hectic, with last-minute ministerial or office meetings for the preparation of briefs. Once we had sailed, however, we were relatively free, for though we could, if necessary, receive telegrams (we sometimes, but not always took cyphers with us) telephoning to and from ships at sea was not then practicable. On this, as on almost all our subsequent voyages together, the Secretary of State began by spending two or three days in bed. This enabled him to recover his energy, and by the time we reached our destination he was usually in pretty good shape. (He was fortunately a good sailor.) Furthermore, he had ample time to look at his briefs and to reflect on the various problems we were going to discuss. I cannot help thinking that politicians who after long journeys by air go directly into important meetings or negotiations are putting themselves at a disadvantage.

On this trip we also had on board not only Hector McNeil* who, like Mr Gromyko, another fellow-passenger, was bound for

* Minister of State at the Foreign Office.

the United Nations, but various other Western Foreign Ministers on their way to Washington for the signing of the Treaty. These included Monsieur Spaak, whom I then partnered at deck tennis and whom I was to get to know very much better in years to come, Dr Stikker of the Netherlands, of whom I also saw a good deal subsequently, and Monsieur Bech, the Luxembourg Minister for Foreign Affairs. Monsieur Bech, a delightful character, had played a key rôle in his country's politics for thirty years or more and now combined the rôle of Minister for 'Viticulture', i.e. wine, about which he was very knowledgeable, with that of Foreign Minister.

When we finally docked at New York the first engagement was a Press Conference on board. This was a chaotic affair with journalists and photographers milling around, all trying to catch the Secretary of State's attention, while he remained quite unperturbed. He told them very little that was new but that did not seem to matter. When the time came to go ashore we were on the lookout for hostile demonstrators or Jewish pickets (for Mr Bevin's Palestine policy had not been forgiven here) but there was no trouble, and, preceded by a motor cycle police escort with screaming sirens which swept the traffic aside, we dashed through the streets of Manhattan to the Pennsylvania station. Mr Bevin did not altogether approve of the traffic being dislocated on his behalf but the New York police (like their Paris counterparts) seemed thoroughly to enjoy conducting distinguished visitors at high speed through the centre of their city. I found these drives rather exhilarating and always admired the skill of the police riders.

When we got to the Embassy at Washington there was inevitably a great accumulation of papers awaiting us and we now embarked on a period of intense activity. The following day we had our first session with Dean Acheson, who had succeeded General Marshall as Secretary of State only two months before, so that Mr Bevin had hitherto had little or no direct contact with him. I had the advantage of having got to know Dean in Washington during the war. Among other things we were both keen participants in the Embassy/State Department games of softball (an amateur's version of baseball) which used to take place on Sunday afternoons.

Our side for the talks consisted only of the Secretary of State

Oliver Franks and myself, which meant that I had to take the record, as on many similar occasions in the future. This meeting was of considerable interest as the Americans told us of the secret exchanges which had just taken place at the United Nations between their representative, Phil Jessup, and the Russian, Malik, which indicated that the Russians might be prepared to do a deal over Berlin which would involve calling off the blockade. The meeting was a long one but Ernie, who at the outset was suspicious of Russian intentions, was reassured by Dean's explanation of how the Americans were handling the negotiations. The drafting of the reporting telegrams to the Foreign Office needed care, for it was important to give an accurate assessment of both the Russian and American attitudes and we wanted a quick and positive reaction from London—which was happily forthcoming.

This meeting and those that followed established a basis of mutual confidence between the two Secretaries of State, who from now on addressed each other as 'Ernie' and 'Dean', or, more frequently, 'me lad'. I was fascinated by the contrast between the two and at the same time relieved to see that a happy relationship was being formed. I also enjoyed seeing Oliver Franks in action. He did not bother about briefs or records and at times seemed somewhat detached, but if, as sometimes happened, the Ministers got into a tangle over some complex problem he had a remarkable gift for sorting out the issues and listing (A, B and C) the possible courses open to them. Even Dean Acheson, who certainly was not lacking in intellectual clarity, used to listen admiringly to these Franks interventions.

We had arrived in Washington on 30 March and the signature ceremony was not until 4 April, but the intervening days were very full, with a series of meetings at the State Department or with other visiting Foreign Ministers, a speech by the Secretary of State at the Washington Press Club, and numerous luncheon and dinner parties.

Ernie Bevin had a notable success at the Press Club where his answers to questions were particularly well received. (When asked about the attitude of the Kremlin, he replied, 'Its mysteries are as dark to me as they are to the alert American pressmen.')

I kept a note of our activities during this period, and our programme for one of these days, Saturday, 2 April, shows the sort of life we led. We started with a meeting of the Foreign Ministers of the Brussels Powers at 9.30, and this was followed by a session with Monsieur Schuman to discuss the future of the Italian colonies at 10 o'clock. We then went straight off to a meeting of all the Atlantic Pact Foreign Ministers and their advisers at which the arrangements for the signature ceremony were discussed and one or two final points cleared up. We returned to a luncheon party at the Embassy for the leaders of the American Federation of Labour, and as soon as that was over we went back to the State Department for a further meeting with Dean Acheson to exchange views on the Middle East and Far Eastern problems. From there we went on to another meeting between Dean Acheson and the Ministers of the Brussels Treaty Powers to discuss, among other things, Indonesia. This went on till nearly 6 o'clock when we returned for a large cocktail party at the Embassy. The Secretary of State had a dinner engagement (and so had I) and half way through the cocktail party I persuaded him to go up to his room for a short rest. I went up to see him when it was time for him to dress for dinner and had to wake him up. I went back a quarter of an hour later, only to find that he had gone to sleep again! He looked up somewhat blearily, saying, 'I'm a naughty boy, aren't I,' and I helped him to dress as rapidly as possible. We eventually got him off, rather late, to his party and I went off to mine. Although the next day was Sunday, we had meetings from 9.30 until midday, when happily there was a free interval until a dinner party at the Embassy in the evening.

At the signature ceremony on 4 April each of the Foreign Ministers was to make a short speech, and as usual there was a frantic rush to complete the Secretary of State's in time. The thoughts it contained were his own, but I had to try, without changing too much, to give them reasonable form. The final result was no literary masterpiece but it was simple and sincere and it is perhaps worth quoting one or two characteristic sentences: 'Countries whose representatives are signing this great pact today are composed of peace-loving peoples with spiritual affinities, but who also have great pride in their skill and their production, and in their achievements in mastering the forces of nature and harnessing the great resources of the world for the benefit of mankind. Our peoples do not glorify war but they will not shrink from it if

aggression is threatened . . . Today . . . is a day of solemn thought
—and, may I say, consecration for peace and resistance to aggression.'

It seemed to me at the time that he received more applause
than any other speaker, and he was warmly congratulated by
President Truman as well as by Dean Acheson. He himself was
in high spirits, for he was convinced that the conclusion of the
Treaty marked a great step forward in the struggle for world peace,
and he was justifiably proud of his contribution. The excitement
of the occasion brought on an angina attack, fortunately not until
he had got back to the Embassy, but after a short rest he was able
to dress and set off for President Truman's dinner party.

I went with other members of our delegation to the reception
which followed the President's party. The American Government
has never seemed to me to be very well organised for the giving
of official hospitality, and this party, which took place in a hotel
and at which, as I noted in a letter home, there was nothing to
eat and only New York State champagne to drink, was a colourless affair compared to what would have been laid on in Paris or
London, or indeed in most of the smaller European capitals, on
such an occasion.

The following day we caught the early morning train to New
York in order to look in at the meeting of the United Nations
Assembly, then in progress at Flushing Meadows. I returned
from the Assembly to do some work at the British Delegation
office which was on the sixty-first floor of the Empire State Building, whence one naturally had a magnificent view of the great city
with its many waterways. After a United Nations cocktail party,
at which I was introduced to the President's daughter, Margaret
Truman, Ernie was host at a dinner for the United Nations
Secretary General, Mr Trygve Lie, and we finally caught the late
night train back to Washington. After two more strenuous days
of meetings at the State Department, devoted largely to the
problems of the Occupying Powers in Germany, we set off again
by train for New York, where, having made our usual dash through
the city with our police escort, we boarded the *Mauretania* half
an hour before she sailed.

The Secretary of State had had an exhausting time, and so
indeed had I. Quite apart from the signing of the Treaty we could

look back on a very productive series of discussions at the State Department. Dean Acheson, in his *Memoirs*, comments that these ten days were a period of considerable achievement and this was undoubtedly the case. For me personally it had been a testing time and I was rather pleased when on the voyage home Ernie observed that I 'seemed to be getting the hang of things'.

Among our fellow-passengers were Arthur Deakin, Mr Bevin's successor at the Transport and General Workers Union, who was a close friend and devoted admirer, and also Gracie and Tommy Fields. They, and others, came to have drinks in the Secretary of State's cabin, and the Fields were naturally the chief stars at the ship's concert.

Our next trip was to Berlin. The Allied discussions with the Russians had been proceeding satisfactorily since our meeting with Dean Acheson in Washington, and on 5 May the Secretary of State was able to inform the House of Commons that agreement had been reached for the lifting of the blockade. This news was greeted with great applause and he received warm congratulations from Winston and others. Meanwhile Berlin was still very short of supplies so that the airlift had to continue, and Ernie was keen to see it in operation. It was decided that we should go to Berlin by special aircraft (a RAF York) the following weekend, and a full programme was hurriedly prepared.

There was a great crowd to greet us at Gatow airfield. We began with a briefing about the organisation of the airlift, after which we drove round and Ernie made short speeches to aircrews and members of the ground staff, congratulating them on their achievements.

Driving through the centre of Berlin down the Kurfürstendamm and to the Brandenburger Tor gave us some impression of the appalling desolation. Very little had yet been rebuilt. I had of course seen the destruction in the City of London, and larger areas of devastation in Budapest, but nothing to compare with this.

The following day was spent partly in visits to the British troops, which involved Ernie saying a few words in sergeants' messes and canteens (which he did very well) and partly in discussions with the German authorities, to whom he gave plenty of frank advice. They had many grave problems but at least there was then no Wall.

We left Berlin in the special aircraft of General Robertson,* the High Commissioner, and went to spend the next night at his Schloss at Ostenwalde in the British zone. There we met a series of German politicians, including Dr Adenauer, then little known outside his own country but an impressive figure whose calm and realistic approach to the problems of the Occupation contrasted with the emotional attitude of some of the others, notably his Socialist rival, Schumacher.

Ten days later we were off again, this time to Paris for a session of the Council of Foreign Ministers, to discuss the situation in Berlin and other German problems. This Conference, which took place at the Palais Rose, an ornate edifice of pink marble, was to last for a month and was almost entirely unproductive.

It had been decreed that this time Mrs Bevin should accompany us, and after much discussion it was decided that she and the Secretary of State would stay at the Plaza Athénée, while the rest of us were to be at the Hotel Bristol. In view of the length of our stay it was just as well that the Secretary of State had declined the offer of accommodation at the Embassy, but in fact he never liked staying at the Paris Embassy whatever the circumstances, and always preferred to be in a hotel. I never discovered whether this was because he had had some disagreeable experience at the Embassy either during the Harvey régime or during that of his predecessor Duff Cooper,† or because he simply preferred to to be more independent. Incidentally, Ernie had been an admirer of Duff Cooper, whose despatches he had found interesting and stimulating, and though Duff's appointment had of course been a political one, Ernie had prolonged his stay in Paris, much to the disgust of some Labour back-benchers.

When Harold Wilson and George Brown, more than twenty years later, appointed another Conservative ex-Cabinet Minister, Christopher Soames, to the Paris Embassy, they were, therefore, to some extent following Ernie's example.

Mrs Bevin's presence during such a long conference was a complicating factor, for she naturally got bored in her hotel room, and was apt to complain to the poor Secretary of State that nobody paid any attention to her. From time to time one of our lady

---

* Subsequently Lord Robertson of Oakridge.
† Later Lord Norwich.

secretaries would be deputed to escort her on a shopping expedition, but this was liable to be a painful experience. What usually happened was that Mrs Bevin would sit down in a chair and ask to see an assortment of wares until half the contents of the shop had been laid out on the counter for her inspection. She would then announce cheerfully that she did not think she would buy anything that day and walk out.

She was always delighted to receive presents and was not above indicating this to foreign hosts. When returning with new acquisitions it never occurred to her, or to Ernie for that matter, that the British Customs were entitled to ask questions. On one occasion, when we were coming back from Strasbourg just before Easter, they had acquired a case of Alsatian wine. The detective who was clearing the luggage was heard saying to the Customs officer as he pointed, with a wink, to the carton of clinking bottles, 'You know, Easter eggs and that sort of thing.'

Mrs Bevin's intentions were doubtless of the best but she never seemed to notice when her husband was tired and wished to be left in peace. She was also quite capable of asking him to move pieces of luggage or even furniture, which was the worst sort of activity for him. So, though on the whole he liked having her around, she was also at times a liability and was prone to upset him either by her complaints or by her demands to be taken out when she knew he had work to do. We Private Secretaries had to watch our step, but she had a kind heart and on the whole relations between us remained good.

I should also like to pay a tribute to the Bevins' married daughter, Queenie Wynne, who was always a great comfort to him and who seemed to understand his needs better than Mrs Bevin. When in London he saw a lot of her but she did not of course come with us on trips abroad.

The Palais Rose sessions were frustrating, as the Russian attitude was almost totally obstructive. The pace was also very slow owing to the need for every statement to be translated twice—the proceedings being conducted in English, French and Russian and there being at that time no provision for simultaneous interpretation. Furthermore, though the objectives of the three Western Ministers were similar, they were liable to have differing views on tactics and from time to time a good deal of heat was engendered by complaints that one of the colleagues had reacted either too violently or not firmly enough to some Russian statement. Dean Acheson lacked the patience of Ernie Bevin and from time to time could not resist letting fly. On one occasion, after a particularly disingenuous statement by Vyshinsky, he addressed the latter as follows: 'Mr Vyshinsky, I should like to adapt an old New England saying and tell you that your last statement was as full of propaganda as a dog is full of fleas—in fact it was all fleas and no dog.' When this had been rather laboriously translated into Russian it evoked a wan smile. A little later Vyshinsky tried to get some of his own back, saying that he would now quote from the Bible for Mr Acheson's edification, and came out with, 'Don't hunt for fleas or the camels will slip through your fingers.'

At one stage Ernie and I plus an interpreter went off for a private meeting with Vyshinsky at the Russian Embassy which lasted for more than two hours. Ernie was rather pleased with the way he had handled Vyshinsky, and said to me afterwards that the latter had reminded him of a cornered rat, but though Vyshinsky had clearly had his hands tied by very strict instructions from Moscow it seemed to me that he was quite capable of talking himself out of most situations.

During our stay in Paris my mind frequently went back to those days in May and June 1940 when we in the Embassy had been preparing for our departure from Paris. The weather this time was by no means as perfect as it had been in that exceptional summer of 1940, but if I had a few hours to spare at a weekend I was sometimes able to visit old haunts. One Sunday afternoon I went for a walk in the Bagatelle Gardens where I had last been with Peter Scarlett,* shortly before his capture by the Germans. On another I went with Ernie to call on Monsieur Blum, the old Socialist leader and former Prime Minister. He had been imprisoned by the Pétain régime following the Riom trials and was now very frail but was clearly delighted to see us. He recalled how he had come to lunch at my flat in Paris in June 1940 and how he had then been still under the illusion that something might be done to prevent the complete collapse of France. He also described to Ernie how I had been to see him in Bordeaux† a day or

* Later Sir Peter Scarlett, Ambassador to Oslo and Minister to the Vatican.   † See p. 136.

two before the Armistice was signed and had conveyed a message encouraging him to come to Britain. He had been much tempted but had decided that it was his duty to stay in France. It was a very understandable decision but in fact he achieved little by staying, whereas if he had come to London he might well have changed the character of the Free French Movement and probably for the better.

After some three weeks of the Conference there was a break while the French and British Ministers went off to Luxembourg for a meeting of the Brussels Treaty Powers. Luxembourg proved a pleasant interlude and we stayed at a comfortable old-fashioned hotel, the Brasseur. I remember being slightly taken aback the first morning when, as I lay in my bath, the portly figure of the Secretary of State suddenly appeared in the doorway demanding the draft of a speech on which I had been working late the night before. At the weekend I managed to take a few hours off for an expedition to an attractive small river where I caught several trout on a dry fly before hurrying back. The same evening there was a splendid party at the Grand Ducal Palace at which we were expected to wear white ties and decorations. Ernie, who had deliberately not brought his tail coat, was a conspicuous figure in his dinner jacket, but this did not worry him, nor, I suspect, the Grand Duchess. I myself had quite a long talk with the Grand Duchess and Prince Felix, not, I must admit, about the political problems of the moment but about sport in Scotland, a country which they knew well.

Shortly after our return to Paris the Conference was brought to a conclusion. A few modest results had been achieved but the main problems were by no means settled and the arguments were to continue for many more dreary months, though not, happily, at ministerial level.

Our final departure was even more chaotic than usual. We were due to catch the night ferry train at 9.30 p.m. at the Gare du Nord, but in the final session the Russians kept on bringing up fresh points, and it looked as though the meeting would never end. We had taken the precaution of asking to have the train held for our benefit, which was just as well as we did not leave the Conference room until 9.25. The drive to the Gare du Nord was accomplished at breakneck speed and we were relieved to see the train still standing at the platform. Our arrival was greeted with applause by an admiring crowd and we proceeded at a stately pace to our reserved coach—for nothing could make Ernie walk fast.

At the end of August we were off again to Washington. This time we were going primarily for 'financial discussions'—which meant in fact that we were going to discuss the impending devaluation of the pound—after which there were to be talks with the State Department about various foreign policy problems before we moved up to New York for the United Nations General Assembly. The Chancellor, Stafford Cripps, and various Treasury advisers were coming for the financial talks, and the immediate party on the *Mauretania* consisted of Mr and Mrs Bevin, Roger Makins and myself on the Foreign Office side, and the Chancellor, Edwin Plowden* and William Armstrong (then the Chancellor's Private Secretary)† from the Treasury. The officials were all good friends, but our two Ministers, who had been constantly opposed in the pre-war struggles within the Labour Party, were still inclined to watch each other with a certain suspicion. It would indeed be difficult to imagine two individuals more unlike than Ernie and Stafford Cripps, in character, upbringing, appearance or general behaviour, and the contrast was often comical.

I had not previously had many dealings with the Chancellor, who, contrary to my expectations, proved rather good company at our table at meals. He annoyed Ernie, however, by wanting to start work on our briefs almost as soon as we sailed, and there were other minor sources of friction. I must admit that on the whole Stafford Cripps, who undoubtedly respected Ernie's great qualities, and realised that he would need his support in Washington, behaved the better of the two—which meant that I had a more difficult job than William Armstrong! Anyhow, between us we succeeded in keeping the two prima donnas in a reasonably co-operative frame of mind.

When we got to Washington the two Ministers and I stayed at the Embassy while the rest of the party went to a hotel. Oliver

* Then Chief Planning Officer, later Chairman of the Atomic Energy Authority, etc. Created Baron Plowden.
† Later Sir William Armstrong, Permanent Secretary to the Treasury, etc., now Lord Armstrong.

Franks and his wife wisely had breakfast in their own room while Ernie, Stafford Cripps and I had ours in the former's sitting room. Stafford had usually got up at about 6 o'clock, had a swim and been for a walk, and by breakfast time he was in hearty form and anxious to get down to business. Ernie, who had generally been to a dinner of some kind the night before (which meant that he had probably consumed a good deal of brandy) and who had not, as in London, had a box of papers to cause him to rise early, did *not* feel merry and bright at breakfast, and showed it very clearly. I had my work cut out to prevent explosions. Incidentally, the Chancellor, who was a vegetarian and was popularly supposed to eat very little at any time, consumed a very hearty breakfast including yoghurt, a peach or half a melon, cereals and cream, and toast and marmalade. Ernie stuck conservatively to eggs and bacon.

The financial discussions were conducted in great secrecy, and I was not normally involved, though I participated in a meeting one night at the Embassy at which we sat round discussing what rate of devaluation to recommend. Once the devaluation issue was out of the way I became heavily engaged. Our programme, as always in Washington, was a strenuous one, involving many meetings at the State Department and frequent late nights, but on the whole the Secretary of State stood up to it very well.

This was the third time in less than six months that we had had detailed talks with Dean Acheson and his officials about the various foreign problems of the moment (the second series having been in Paris in June) and this helps to illustrate how close Anglo-American relations were at that moment. The 'special relationship' was then very much a reality and I do not think anyone else was the worse for it. Other members of the Western Alliance, including in particular the French, were from time to time brought into the discussions, but a basic Anglo-American understanding was a pre-requisite for progress. The Germans and the Japanese had not, of course, as yet re-emerged on the scene, and the rôle of Italy was still a relatively minor one.

The last ten days of September were spent in New York, where we stayed at the Waldorf Astoria. The Secretary of State worked mostly in the hotel, where the Achesons were also staying, but we made periodic excursions to the United Nations Assembly at

Flushing Meadows, and in addition I had from time to time to look in at our Delegation office in the Empire State Building.

One night I was with the Secretary of State in the Achesons' suite when the news came through that the Russians had success-fully exploded an atomic bomb. This was much earlier than the experts had predicted, and caused a considerable sensation—and a good deal of gloom. We had to take quick decisions on what our public reaction should be.

The Secretary of State's speech at the United Nations Assembly was a major event which kept us all busy throughout the preced-ing weekend, and there were other speeches to be made at lun-cheons and dinners which added to the burden—though these were mostly 'ex tempor'. We also tended to have late-night sessions, and one such meeting with Acheson, Schuman and Vyshinsky went on until 2.45 a.m., by which time tempers were getting decidedly frayed.

Both in Washington and in New York Mike Pearson, then Canadian Secretary of State for External Affairs (whom I had previously known when he was second in command at the Canadian Embassy in Washington), had tended to be increasingly involved in our discussions, and at the end of the month we went up to Ottawa for talks with the Canadians. Ottawa was a very pleasant change after the heat and turmoil of New York and the Canadians were excellent hosts. On our return journey we went by car from Ottawa to Montreal, where the Secretary of State addressed the Canada Club, and we later caught the night train to New York. It had been a brilliantly fine day and the fall colours—reds, golds and different shades of green—were a marvellous sight.

On 6 October we thankfully embarked on the *Queen Elizabeth* after a month of pretty well non-stop activity which would have taxed the powers of a younger and healthier man than the Secre-tary of State.

In November we were in Paris again for meetings of the Council of Europe and the Brussels Treaty Powers and for further talks with the Americans and the French about Germany. Whereas the Secretary of State had great faith in NATO, which he now regarded as one of the corner-stones of the security of the Western World, he had many reservations about the Council of Europe, the proper rôle of which never seemed to him to have been satisfactorily established. His attitude was indicated by his famous observation: 'If you open that Pandora's Box you never know what Trojan 'orses will jump out.' Another characteristic remark, provoked by an argument over the respective rôles of the Council of Ministers and the Assembly, was as follows: 'I am not a very strong believer in Constitutions. I like the thing that grows, the thing that evolves.'

This time the Secretary of State stayed with the rest of us at the Hotel Bristol where he and Mrs Bevin occupied the Penthouse Suite. It was a great inconvenience to be under the same roof, particularly as there were frequent late-night sessions.

Our next major outing was to Colombo, for a meeting of the Foreign Ministers of all the independent members of the Commonwealth (of which there were then only eight). There had been meetings of Commonwealth Prime Ministers before this but it was the first time that the Foreign Ministers—or Ministers for External Affairs—had come together. This was one of the reasons why Ernie Bevin, who was a great believer in the potentialities of the Commonwealth (in its form at that time), attached particular importance to this gathering. We left home on Boxing Day, 1949, and after a pause in Paris for dinner at the Embassy we set off by the night train for Rome. We spent the next night at the Embassy there before flying on by RAF plane to Malta, where we had lunch with the Governor, and thence to Fayid, the British base in the Canal Zone. The Secretary of State had not been well when we started and was in pretty poor shape throughout this part of the journey, but fortunately we had Alec McCall with us so I was relieved of the main responsibility for his health.

At Suez we went aboard HMS *Kenya*. She was to drop us off at Colombo on her way to the Far East, and both the Secretary of State and I had been looking forward to this part of the journey. He did not look at all well as we went on board, and some of the officers confided to me afterwards that they had discussed among themselves whether he could be expected to survive the journey. As usual, however, a few days in bed and plenty of sun and sea air worked wonders, and by the time we emerged from the Red Sea into the Indian Ocean he was looking a different man.

The Secretary of State, Alec McCall and I were established in great comfort in the accommodation aft normally reserved for an Admiral, where we had our own dining room and sitting room. Michael Wilford and our secretaries, together with the rest of the Delegation, which included Philip Noel-Baker and officials from the Commonwealth Relations Office and the Treasury as well as the Foreign Office, were proceeding direct to Colombo by air.

HMS *Kenya* was newly commissioned, and though minor things were apt to go wrong I was impressed by the prevailing atmosphere of keenness. We for our part led a wonderfully lazy life, eating, sleeping, reading and spending a lot of time sitting in the sun.

One day the Secretary of State was invited to address the ship's company assembled on the quarterdeck, and he asked me to jot down a rough outline for the sort of review of world problems which I had often heard him give elsewhere. The main theme was to be that we had got to resist aggression wherever it might threaten. He followed my notes pretty closely, but at one stage inserted a passage, saying, out of the blue, that he was very worried about the precarious situation in Korea. At that time Korea had been quite out of the news for many months, and there were no signs of impending trouble. Ernie's anxieties were however all too well-founded, for less than six months later the Korean war had begun, and HMS *Kenya* was to find herself engaged in hostilities in Korean waters. The Secretary of State's prophetic remark had made an impression on some of the officers, from whom I subsequently heard when they were, as they observed, 'resisting aggression' off the Korean coast.

In the evenings there were entertainments of various kinds, a dinner in the Wardroom, film shows, and a ship's concert with plenty of broad humour which Ernie thoroughly enjoyed. There was one particularly fine evening when the Secretary of State, the doctor and I were entertained by all the officers to a very splendid dinner on the quarterdeck. I believe this involved changing course to ensure that we were not too blown about.

Ernie, who by now had won the respect and admiration of all, made a most entertaining speech which just suited the occasion.

On the night before our arrival in Colombo we decided to give a return dinner party in the Admiral's dining room, and invited the Captain and as many of the other senior officers as we could fit in. The doctor and I planned the menu and the wines to go with it with some care, both of us being particularly anxious that the Secretary of State should not overdo it, and consequently arrive in Colombo in bad shape. We knew that if a decanter of port was left in front of Ernie as host, his glass would be filled all too frequently, so we instructed the Goanese steward that there should be no port but that everyone should be offered brandy. Unfortunately, our instructions were not fully understood, for when everyone had had their glass of brandy the bottle was put down in front of the Secretary of State. The doctor and I looked at each other, but matters were now out of our control and our worst fears were realised as the Secretary of State poured himself out glass after glass. The immediate effect was splendid and Ernie was at the top of his form with an endless stream of anecdotes and stories. Needless to say, however, next morning he was in very poor shape indeed and half the good of the sea voyage seemed to have been lost. As the weather on arrival in Colombo was hot and sticky he felt all the worse.

It had been arranged that the Secretary of State and his immediate party should stay with the Prime Minister, Mr Senanayake, at his delightful house, Temple Trees. Michael Wilford and I shared a suite in the very luxurious guest house adjoining the main residence, and we looked out onto a splendid garden full of brilliant tropical flowers. We were wonderfully looked after, and I reported in a letter home that we were called in the morning with tea, bananas, fresh pineapple and paw paw, to be followed half an hour later by breakfast, consisting of grapefruit, porridge, fish and then eggs. (This of course made a greater impression then, when we had so recently left food-rationing behind us, than it might now.)

Ernie was very keen that something practical should come out of the Conference, for the holding of which he was so largely responsible. His primary objective was to find some way to raise the standard of living in the countries of South and South-East Asia, and he was feeling after some sort of Marshall Plan for the area. The problems were vast and complicated and not all the Governments represented were particularly cooperative, but in the end, under pressure from the British Delegation and with help from the Canadians, there emerged what was to be known as the Colombo Plan.

The Conference sessions were held in a first-floor room and the

F

Ceylonese authorities, conscious of Ernie's infirmity, had arranged for him to be carried up the stairs in a splendid palanquin. This delighted the Press at the opening session, but Ernie felt that he looked foolish and that too much publicity was being given to his state of health. In future he insisted on walking up to the conference room.

Apart from Mr Bevin the outstanding personalities at the conference were Mr Nehru (who was accompanied by his daughter, Mrs Indira Gandhi, the future Prime Minister) and Mike Pearson. These three were given honorary degrees at Colombo University. Degree Day was quite an interesting occasion but Ernie did not like having to wear a gown and was generally unenthusiastic. It had happily been agreed that there should be only one speech on behalf of the recipients, and that this should be made by Mr Nehru. It was clear when he began that he had not prepared his speech at all, and the introduction was scrappy and halting. Once he was properly launched, however, he gave a brilliant talk, in his impeccable English, on the rôle of youth in confronting the problems of the day.

One evening, after a small dinner with the Governor General, I found myself sitting beside Mr Nehru on a sofa. He was clearly tired and had no wish to discuss the Conference or politics, but he warmed up slightly when I got him onto the subject of Harrow and his friendship there with Field Marshal Alexander, who was an exact contemporary and in the same House.

After a strenuous week of meetings and official entertainment it was decided to have a break at the weekend, and we arranged to go up to Kandy. Roger Makins came with us and we joined up with the Mike Pearsons. We visited the very fine Peradinya botanical gardens and were taken to see elephants bathe in a river. As Ernie stood surveying them one could not help thinking that there were certain resemblances—the same plodding step and rolling gait, as well as a sense of humour and a very long memory.

The afternoon was devoted to a visit to the famous Temple of the Tooth (which is supposed to house one of Buddha's teeth). The tooth, which is reputed to have supernatural healing powers, is normally only exposed to view once or twice a year on special occasions, but the Ceylonese were happy that there should be an unveiling for Mr Bevin's benefit, and he himself was very keen to see 'the tuth', as he called it. We none of us had any idea what form the ceremony would take, but having been received by the priests of the temple we soon found ourselves following in procession to the inner sanctum where the tooth was kept in a series of jewel-studded caskets. As the procession moved along to the chanting of the priests it became clear that there were several flights of steps to be climbed, and Alec McCall, who disapproved of the whole proceedings, was heard muttering, 'This will surely kill him.' Ernie, however, was thoroughly enjoying himself and nothing would stop him until we had witnessed the unveiling of the tooth. As we slowly ascended the stairs, having previously removed our shoes, those following noted with amusement that Ernie had an enormous hole in the heel of one of his socks. During the ceremony of unveiling the tooth, which incidentally is a monster fang and certainly does not look human, Ernie was heard to say in a loud aside as he contemplated all the gold and precious stones, 'They'd look better out, they don't know we 'ave someone from our Treasury 'ere who would like to get 'is 'ands on some of that stuff.' Fortunately, in spite of the doctor's apprehensions Ernie emerged none the worse, and though the tooth had not effected a miraculous cure, the weekend outing and the cooler atmosphere of Kandy had certainly had a beneficial effect.

When, thanks largely, as I have said, to the endeavours of the British Delegation, the Conference had been brought to quite a successful conclusion we embarked again in another cruiser, HMS *Birmingham*, then on her homeward journey after two years in the Far East. We again had the Admiral's quarters and enjoyed an extremely comfortable and restful life like that on HMS *Kenya* with only an occasional telegram requiring attention.

In the evenings there were usually entertainments of one kind or another, and the time passed all too quickly. We stopped off at Aden, where we did a little sightseeing, and also received a bag containing papers, which meant that from then onwards there was rather more work to be done. When, towards the end of this trip, we again entertained the Captain and some of his senior officers, the doctor's and my precautions worked according to plan and only a limited amount of brandy was consumed. Accordingly, by the time we reached Suez the Secretary of State was in quite good shape and ready for what were to be some arduous days of talks with the Egyptians in Cairo.

We stayed in great comfort with Ronnie Campbell* at the Cairo Embassy, the lawns of which then ran down to the bank of the Nile, where I believe a new road has since been built. Prince Philip, then a Naval Lieutenant, and the Commander-in-Chief, Mediterranean, also happened to be guests of the Ambassador (which incidentally posed certain problems of protocol) and we were all invited to a Lucullan lunch by King Farouk. The latter's looks were very much against him but he was quite a good host and the atmosphere was relaxed.

Our talks with Nahas Pasha, who was then Prime Minister, and his Foreign Minister, Salah-el-Din, were not very productive. Looking back I suppose that our respective objectives were irreconcilable. Nothing less than the complete and unconditional evacuation of Egyptian territory by British forces plus what the Egyptians termed 'the unity of the Nile Valley'—which meant the right to bring the Sudan under the Egyptian crown—would have been acceptable to the Egyptian politicians, and we were not then prepared to concede either.

Our official programme allowed a little time for sightseeing—a visit to the Citadel and a drive out to the Pyramids and the Sphinx. It was a brilliantly fine but chilly day, and Ernie enjoyed it. He did not, like his successor, Alec Douglas-Home, try riding a camel—it would indeed have been a remarkable sight if he had—but he was greatly interested in what he saw. Our Egyptian guide, who was extremely loquacious, ended up his piece on the Sphinx with an eloquent passage about lying there for so many thousands of years silent in the desert, which caused Ernie to observe, 'I see, and now you're trying to make up for lost time on 'is behalf.'

On leaving Cairo we drove down to Alexandria where we were picked up by HMS *Birmingham* and taken to Naples, whence we went by road to Rome. It was quite a cavalcade, with escorting police cars, and at the outset there was a minor commotion when some Neapolitan Communists threw rotten eggs at the ambassadorial Rolls in which Ernie was travelling. Later on an incident occurred which shocked both Ernie and me. A flock of sheep was crossing the road ahead of us and the first police car drove straight

* Sir Ronald I. Campbell, Ambassador to Egypt.

through the tail end of it without making any effort to stop, leaving several dead or dying bodies by the roadside.

We spent one night in Rome and were entertained at a dinner given by Count Sforza at the Villa Madama. He made a speech in the course of which he expressed the hope that the United Kingdom would give a moral lead in Europe. This thoroughly annoyed Ernie who drew attention to all that Britain had done since the end of the war to assist the recovery of Western Europe, and implied that it was time others did a bit more to help.

While in Rome we also went to call on the Pope—a novel experience for the anti-Catholic Ernie. I am sure that he and the next Pope, John XXIII, whom I was to meet at a later date, would have got on particularly well together. Pope Pius XII was much more reserved but Ernie seemed quite pleased with the outcome of their private session and we were all received most benevolently.

During the next few months we went to two meetings of the Council of Europe in Strasbourg and to Brussels Treaty sessions in Paris, Brussels and The Hague. Ernie had been enthusiastic about the choice of Strasbourg as the seat of the Council of Europe, hoping that it would become a symbol of Franco-German reconciliation. But he did not much like the place when we got there and on our second visit we stayed in a hotel up in the Vosges where the atmosphere was certainly less oppressive. In Brussels we stayed at the recently acquired British Embassy in the Rue Ducale which I was later to get to know so well. As I often pointed out to our guests in years to come, there was a particularly narrow door, leading from the bedroom which Ernie occupied to the adjoining sitting room, through which his bulky frame was unable to pass either forwards or sideways.

All these trips were of relatively short duration and our only other major expedition after Colombo was a visit to New York and Washington in September 1950. Ernie had been none too well and people were beginning to question more openly whether he would be able to carry on much longer as Foreign Secretary. He, however, saw very clearly that much still remained to be done to consolidate the Western Alliance, and he believed that he was better qualified than anyone else to ensure its continued development. There were so many matters to which he had devoted his energies and which he wished to see carried a stage further, that, though conscious of his failing strength, he could not bear the idea of handing over to a successor.

There was to be a meeting of the Atlantic Council in New York, followed by tripartite talks with the French and Americans on Germany, after which the Secretary of State was to address the General Assembly of the United Nations. On 7 September we embarked once more on the *Queen Mary* with a powerful team, including Ivone Kirkpatrick, who was then High Commissioner in Germany. Among our fellow-passengers were various other Foreign Ministers bound for the United Nations. We stayed at the Waldorf Astoria and had the usual strenuous New York programme. The meetings of the Atlantic Council were concerned in particular with the problem of German rearmament and this was such a delicate issue that Ernie decided that the Minister of Defence, Emmanuel Shinwell, must be summoned from London to share the responsibility for the decisions which were clearly going to be necessary. Though Ernie accepted that there was a convincing case for bringing in the Germans, he did not much relish the prospect and this produced some unusually obscure pronouncements from him. On one occasion Dean Acheson, who was becoming a trifle impatient, was moved to say 'If Mr Bevin means what I think he means but not what he said, we are in agreement.'

Mrs Bevin had come with us on this trip, and apart from the official meetings there was a considerable amount of social activity. One evening I went with the Bevins, the Achesons and the Mike Pearsons to the Sadlers Wells Ballet with Margot Fonteyn, which was then at the Metropolitan Opera, and I also had a chance to see *South Pacific* which was the great musical hit of the moment. The Bevins also went to lunch one day with Eleanor Roosevelt and saw over the Roosevelt home at Hyde Park.

The Secretary of State's major speech at the United Nations Assembly was a good one, and very well received. As usual, the ideas were his but I had to re-write it fairly extensively.

All things considered, Ernie got through this strenuous period very well, though not without a good deal of pain. We were all pretty exhausted by the time we were due to return, and were glad to embark once more on our return journey on 29 September.

On these many trips overseas I got to know Ernie in a way that would never have been possible had we remained in London. When at the Foreign Office there were occasions, usually at the end of the day or on a Saturday afternoon, when Ernie would relax and like to chat after asking me to get a bottle and glasses out of the cupboard in his desk, but the normal programme allowed little opportunity to talk about anything but the affairs of the moment. When we were abroad, however, things were very different. Though there were periods of intensive and exhausting activity, there were also times, notably on our various sea voyages, when we were not under pressure. I had many *tête-à-tête* meals with him, and provided that he was feeling reasonably well, these were invariably an entertaining experience. He loved to talk and I was very ready to listen, and used to encourage him to go on by question or comment. Much of the conversation was inevitably about the people we were meeting, our recent experiences or future plans, but I was given a good insight into his attitude to all the problems of the day as well as learning much about his past. The better I got to know and understand him, the greater my admiration.

4

MR BEVIN: SOME GENERAL
COMMENTS AND REFLECTIONS

I HAVE EARLIER mentioned my doubts about my suitability for
the demanding job of Private Secretary. One of my special
anxieties was whether I would ever succeed in establishing a close
and easy relationship with a Secretary of State whose background,
early life and education, not to mention his subsequent career, had
been so totally different from my own. As most readers will probably know, Ernie Bevin had never known his father, or indeed who
his father was. (The register of births at Winsford in Somerset has
a blank in the space for name of father.) He was the seventh child
of his mother, Mercy Bevin, who had formerly been married to a
farm labourer and who later worked as a village midwife and inter-
mittently as a domestic servant. She died when he was six years
old and he then went to live with his married sister. He left school
and began work when he was eleven. He was paid 6s 6d a quarter!
His education had later been continued at night schools (one was
a Quaker Adult School) and through correspondence courses. It
seemed to me that the sheltered life I had led, and an educational
background of Harrow and Trinity, might prove something of a
barrier.

I need not have worried. Harold Caccia,* then my immediate
chief, to whom I had mentioned my misgivings, assured me that
a public school background was no disadvantage with Ernie. After
all, he observed, Ernie had picked on him to be responsible for the
organisation and staffing of the new Foreign Service, and 'nobody
could be more wrapped up in his old school tie' than he was. In
fact, as I was soon to find out, Ernie Bevin was a warm admirer
of Eton and Harrow. He had been to speak at both and had been
favourably impressed by what he saw and by his reception from

* Later Ambassador in Washington, Permanent Under Secretary at
the Foreign Office, Provost of Eton, etc.; created Lord Caccia.

76

the boys. He periodically told me that I was extremely lucky to have had the educational opportunities that had come my way, and wished that he had had the same good fortune. He seemed, however, to bear no resentment at having had such a harsh upbringing, and in a way I think that he was all the prouder of having achieved so much after such an unpromising start in life. I dare say that at an earlier stage in his career he may have felt differently, but by the time I came to work with him he was certainly not jealous of anyone, and had attained complete freedom from any social or other prejudices. He treated all men as equals.

Ernie Bevin retained a special feeling of affection for the British working class whom he referred to as 'my people'. He was proud of the great improvements that had been made in social conditions, health and education in this country since the days of his boyhood, and he often referred to these achievements when speaking to audiences in North America. He enjoyed talking to miners' gatherings or indeed to any Trade Union group. But though he had retained a few special friends in his own Union—like Arthur Deakin —I had the impression that the demanding life of a Minister, whether in wartime or in the immediate post-war period, had tended to cut him off from friends of earlier days. The very few people outside political or official circles whose hospitality he was happy to accept were rather an odd assortment.

If there was one group of people whom Ernie disliked and mistrusted it was the Left Wing Intellectuals in his own Party—people like Harold Laski, Kingsley Martin, John Strachey or Crossman. Stafford Cripps, who might have been thought to fall into the same category and had at one stage been an opponent, was, as I have previously mentioned, now tolerated because Ernie respected his intelligence and his integrity. Hugh Gaitskell had to watch his step as a ministerial colleague, and relations were never altogether easy, but on the whole he seemed to be accepted as being a realist and not too dogmatic or doctrinaire. Herbert Morrison, on the other hand, though clearly on the Right of the Labour Party and scarcely to be described as an intellectual, was always an object of suspicion and dislike. This was perhaps regrettable, for Morrison was a key member of the Labour Government and would, I think, have been happy to be on good terms, but the fact was that Ernie did not trust him and he always maintained that there had been occasions in the past when Morrison's conduct had been devious and un-reliable.

Among the junior Ministers at the Foreign Office, the enthusi-astic and devoted Philip Noel-Baker was classified as an intellectual and was treated pretty roughly, and so, though to a lesser degree, was Pakenham.* Chris Mayhew on the other hand escaped the opprobrium of intellectualism and was rather a favourite. Hector McNeil was the closest to Ernie of the Foreign Office junior Ministers, and besides sharing his general approach to the prob-lems of the day, could, I think, be classed as a real friend. Ernie also had a very warm feeling for Lord Henderson, who was Parlia-mentary Under Secretary and Foreign Office spokesman in the House of Lords.

With the possible exception of Hector McNeil, Ernie's political colleagues in the Foreign Office had very little influence on his policies. Though they were given opportunities to express their views their proposals or recommendations were usually looked at by Ernie with a critical eye and were never accepted without having first been subjected to scrutiny by the experts. His likeable Parlia-mentary Private Secretary, Percy Wells, was a useful source of information about opinion among the back-benchers, but he never sought to intervene in questions of foreign policy.

A Ministerial colleague with whom Ernie was almost always on bad terms was Nye Bevan. There was a well-known occasion when the latter had incurred Ernie's displeasure, and one of those present, seeking to excuse Nye, observed that he was sometimes his own worst enemy. 'Not while I'm alive 'e aint!' retorted Ernie. One day when Nye had made a very eloquent speech in the House of Commons and had been complimented by the Press on his oratorical success, I asked Ernie what he had thought of it. 'It sounded as though 'e'd swallowed a dictionary,' said Ernie. ''E used a lot of words but 'e didn't know what they all meant.' Another such speech he dismissed scornfully as 'nothing but clitch after clitch' (i.e. cliché). The fact was that Ernie mistrusted oratory and was not really interested in philosophical argument. He was not so much concerned with doctrines and ideologies as with get-ting things done. His socialism was of a very pragmatic kind, and though he followed certain basic principles and clung to certain

* Now Lord Longford.

ideals, his concern was to find fair and just solutions without worrying too much about their theoretical justification. He had never been a Marxist and had always regarded Communism as a vicious and dangerous creed.

A colleague with whom Ernie had a good deal to do during my time with him was A. V. Alexander, then Minister of Defence. Alexander was a friend of long standing and a devoted admirer. During the Peace Conference in Paris he had sometimes been roped in to play the piano at the sing-songs which Ernie inaugurated for members of the British Delegation and which he greatly enjoyed. But Ernie had a low opinion of Alexander's intellectual capacity and tended to treat him very much as a subordinate. It was sometimes almost embarrassing at meetings to hear Ernie telling such a relatively senior Cabinet colleague in such dictatorial terms just what he should do, but Alexander usually obeyed and did not seem to resent the way he was treated. His successor, Shinwell, a man of very different stamp, was handled by Ernie with much greater circumspection.

There is no doubt that of all the members of the Government Mr Attlee held a special place in Ernie's esteem. They were of course totally unlike—in social background, appearance, and character, the one modest, laconic and at first sight unimpressive, the other extrovert, imaginative, temperamental and making an immediate impact on all with whom he came in contact. In an earlier chapter I mentioned that two of the qualities which Ernie said he took for granted when I was recommended to him were reliability and loyalty, and there is no doubt that he attached the highest importance to both. As a colleague in the War Cabinet he had learnt to appreciate Attlee's complete reliability, and when, after the Labour victory in July 1945, there were some who questioned Attlee's suitability for the leadership, Ernie Bevin, who, if he had wished might have been a candidate for it himself, had no doubt at all that Attlee must be the new Prime Minister. And just as he himself had always been rock-like in his loyalty to Churchill, so from now on he remained absolutely firm in his support of Attlee. When in 1947 Dr Dalton and others plotted to make Ernie Bevin Prime Minister in place of Attlee he refused with indignation to have anything to do with their plans. Fortified, no doubt, by such past experiences, Attlee and he had complete confidence in each other. Ernie was scrupulous about consulting the Prime Minister on all important decisions, and he knew that he could almost invariably get full backing from him for whatever he wanted to do. We have had plenty of examples in the last thirty-five years of friction between the Foreign Secretary and the Prime Minister, and the Attlee–Bevin combination was quite exceptionally trouble-free. This of course made it all the harder for Attlee to insist, as he finally had to do, that Ernie was not physically fit enough to carry on any longer as Foreign Secretary.

Whether in fact Ernie would have liked to be Prime Minister I am not quite sure. He would certainly not have doubted his own ability to do the job, and perhaps, before his health began to fail, he would have been ready in certain circumstances to take it on. If he had, his Foreign Secretary would certainly have had a hard life.

Ernie undoubtedly felt stronger loyalty towards his old Trade Union colleagues than towards the Labour Party as a whole. When, as sometimes happened, he failed to appear at the Foreign Office at the expected time after lunch, we usually discovered that he had gone off to Transport House for a gossip. Sometimes it was to see Arthur Deakin, sometimes to do a little work with his faithful political secretary, Ivy Saunders, who dealt with his constituency business. He still exerted great influence in his own Union, and Arthur Deakin constantly sought his advice, which was given in clear and forthright language. Incidentally, Ernie would, I am convinced, have been often shocked by the behaviour of the Transport and General Workers Union in recent years. The attitude of its members to national issues has altered so much since his day as to be scarcely recognisable. But then he would have been greatly concerned by the state of the whole British Trade Union Movement today.

Among members of the Opposition Ernie got on particularly well with Anthony Eden, and each had a high regard for the other. Alec Cadogan has recorded that after the Conservative defeat in 1945 Eden wrote to him saying, 'I am very glad that Bevin is to be my successor. He is the best man they have.' Ernie had frequently backed Anthony Eden against Winston in the arguments about foreign affairs in the War Cabinet, and had also taken a constructive interest in the Eden proposals for the reform of the Foreign Service in 1943.

Ernie had been a warm admirer of Churchill's leadership during the war years and had consistently supported him publicly when under attack. A notable instance of this had occurred during the Greek crisis in the winter of 1944. The Government's policy, which involved supporting the monarchy in Greece and opposing the left-wing EAM was highly unpopular with a large part of the Labour Party—as with the United States Government. Ernie's approach was typically pragmatic and un-doctrinaire, and his forthright defence of British policy carried much weight. By all accounts Churchill greatly valued Ernie's solid good sense, even though, as mentioned above, there were occasions when the latter was quite prepared to stand up to him in the War Cabinet. By the time I joined Ernie, however, he had become somewhat critical of Winston's incursions into foreign affairs, which he often regarded as mischievous, particularly in the context of the Council of Europe. He also seemed to resent, rather unreasonably, the honours with which Winston was received whenever he went abroad.

Ernie rather liked Rab Butler, and I believe the feeling was mutual. On the other hand Harold Macmillan's voice used to irritate Ernie, and when Macmillan was acting as Conservative spokesman on foreign affairs Ernie became noticeably more combative.

The Bevin–Beaverbrook relationship was a curious and complicated one. At the beginning of the war Beaverbrook had had a high opinion of Ernie's qualities. But they had later had frequent arguments, usually on manpower problems, and when the conflict between the two became acute Churchill felt bound to back Ernie. In 1942, when Beaverbrook was at odds with Churchill as a result of his Press campaign for an early second front, he apparently toyed with the idea of backing Ernie to head a new Government. I more than once heard Ernie recount how Beaverbrook had tried, by exerting all his charm, to win him over to the idea of forming an anti-Churchill clique. Needless to say, Ernie would have none of this and ever after remained deeply suspicious of Beaverbrook —and of his newspapers. The latter in turn tended to criticise Bevin's foreign policies, and when in due course Herbert Morrison succeeded to the Foreign Office, Beaverbrook seems to have believed, very misguidedly, that this would be a change for the better.

Though there were occasions when Ernie clashed with the Opposition in Parliament, his conduct of British foreign policy had from the outset been basically bi-partisan, and criticism came more frequently from the Labour left-wingers than from the Conservative benches. He enjoyed a wide measure of support in the country as a whole, irrespective of party. His robust attitude in the face of Russian pressures and his stalwart defence of British interests in general were welcomed by the great majority of his fellow-countrymen. His reactions to the machinations of foreigners were increasingly accepted as being typically British. Many staunch Conservatives were surprised to find an ex-Trade Union leader, who after all had made his name in battles with the employers, now appearing as a sort of cross between St George and John Bull.

Ernie's first introduction to a group of Foreign Office officials had been at Potsdam, when, as the new Foreign Secretary, he found himself having to pick up the threads half way through the Conference. First impressions on both sides were favourable. Attlee left him to do nearly all the talking in the tripartite meetings, and he at once showed that he was well able to hold his own with both Russians and Americans. In his *Diary* Alec Cadogan* recorded his impressions of his new chief as follows: 'He knows a good deal, is prepared to read any amount, seems to take in what he does read and is capable of making up his own mind and sticking up for his (or our) point of view against anyone.' Not a bad summary of Ernie's qualities as British representative at international meetings.

On one occasion at Potsdam he asked at a meeting of the British Delegation for a problem to be explained to him in miners' language, whereupon the official concerned is reputed to have replied, 'Of course, Secretary of State, if you prefer me to call a spade a bloody shovel I gladly will.' By the end of the Conference he had formed a pretty favourable impression of his new staff and they of him.

In his treatment of his officials in the Foreign Office Ernie was totally unmoved by social origins or supposed political leanings. A few, no doubt, would have qualified for the unpopular category of 'Left Wing Intellectual', but Ernie was concerned only with their effectiveness and their ability to help implement his policies.

* Sir Alexander Cadogan, Permanent Under Secretary of State at the Foreign Office.

He was anxious to see recruitment to the Service open to all, irrespective of social or educational background, and was satisfied that the post-war system had achieved this. But he realised that it would take time for the new policy to affect the upper ranks and in the meanwhile the fact that the majority of the senior members of the Office (though by no means all) had been to one of the great public schools worried him not at all.

Throughout my period as Private Secretary the Permanent Under Secretary was William Strang whom Ernie greatly respected and liked. There is no doubt that he found it much easier to work with William than with his cynical, pessimistic and unconstructive though very likeable predecessor, 'Moley' Sargent.* Ernie equally had a high regard for the two senior Deputy Under Secretaries, Roger Makins and Gladwyn Jebb,† two strong characters with decided views which they were always encouraged to put forward. They in return were warm admirers of the Secretary of State and both took great delight in his comments on men and affairs. Other senior officials whom Ernie always greeted with particular warmth included Bill Dening,‡ Michael Wright,§ Rob Scott‖ and Edmund Hall Patch.¶ The latter amused Ernie by his sartorial eccentricities and was regarded, not without some justice, as a professional pessimist. When someone remarked that so and so was optimistic about finding a solution for some current problem, Ernie interjected, 'Optimist is 'e? Send for 'all-Patch. 'E'll chill 'is bones!'

There were one or two members of the Office who tended to irritate him by their inability to explain a problem clearly or for some other such failing. But he very seldom spoke roughly to any of his officials and if anyone had made a mistake and admitted it he was quickly forgiven. In general all were treated rather as a benevolent uncle might treat some promising nephew who had talent but still

* Sir Orme Sargent.

† Later United Kingdom Permanent Representative to the United Nations, Ambassador at Paris, etc. Created Lord Gladwyn.

‡ Sir Esler Dening, later Ambassador to Japan.

§ Sir Michael Wright, later Ambassador to Norway and Iraq.

‖ Sir Robert H. Scott, later Commissioner General in South-East Asia and Permanent Secretary, Ministry of Defence.

¶ Sir Edmund Hall-Patch, later United Kingdom Representative to OEEC, etc.

a good deal to learn about the ways of the world. Indeed, Gladwyn and others used always to refer to him as Uncle Ernie.

By the time I came on the scene Ernie had made a deep impression on the Service as a whole, and even those in distant posts who had never had any personal dealings with him were conscious of his impact. It was not only that they felt that he cared for their welfare and wished to improve their conditions, or that he had shown his readiness to stand up for members of the Service against any criticism. It was also comforting to know that our foreign policy was now laid down in the Foreign Office—and not at Number 10 or elsewhere—and that once the Foreign Secretary was persuaded of the rightness of a given course it was unlikely that he would fail to get it endorsed by the Cabinet. There was, furthermore, throughout the Service, great confidence in the basic soundness of his judgment and admiration for the way in which he defended essential British interests.

The suggestion that Ernie was in the hands of his Foreign Office officials shows a complete misunderstanding of his character. He had a very strong will, normally knew just what he wanted and had very clear ideas about ministerial responsibility. Though he was always open to argument it was very difficult to persuade him to do something if his instincts were against it. It was slightly easier to head him off some course which he had in mind to follow, and he never resented it if I expressed doubt or disapproval of some project of his. Occasionally, when there had been an outburst of temper—never incidentally directed at me, though from time to time I was the witness of such explosions—I was successful in getting him to hold his hand until he had cooled off. In the heat of the moment he would sometimes dash off an angry letter which I knew would only cause trouble, and I would then suggest that he should sleep on it and look at it again in the morning. This simple expedient usually had the desired effect.

Ernie got on particularly well with George VI for whom he had a warm regard. He was most punctilious about keeping the King informed about what was going on in the field of foreign affairs. On various occasions when I saw them together Ernie would put a large hand on the King's back and lead him to a corner where he would tell him some story which usually evoked roars of laughter.

JSB

Brook and PRUDENCE Bristol

E.B earning 10/- a week as a van-boy.

1. Ernest Bevin's early life in Bristol, as described by himself to Jean (see p. 45).

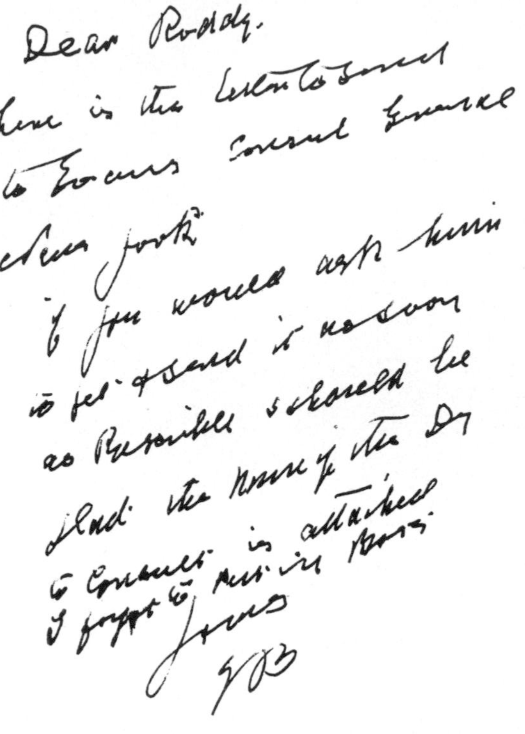
1 CARLTON GARDENS,
LONDON, S.W. 1

WHItehall: 8440
Extn. 653

Dear Roddy.
here is the letter to send
to Evans Consul General
New York
if you would ask him
to get & send it as soon
as possible I should be
glad the name of the Dr
to consult is attached
I forgot to put in box
Yours
E B

(Translation)

Dear Roddy,
here is the letter to senc
Evans Consul General New Yc
if you would ask him to
and send it as soon as possib
should be glad the name of
Dr. to consult is attached I fo
to put in box
Yours
E B
(note. This referred to some m
cine which was then only obt
able in the U.S.A.)

Left 2. A typical sample of Er
Bevin's handwriting (see p. 36

Below 3. Ernest Bevin talking
fidentially to Robert Schuma
the State Department with
author to interpret (see p. 57).

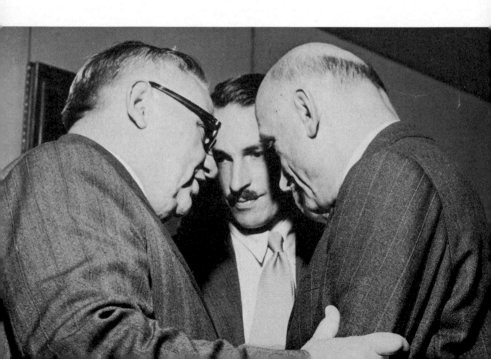

4. M. Bech, Luxembourg Minister for Foreign Affairs (and wine!), greeting the Bevins with M. Schuman and the author at the airport (see p. 63).

5. Ernest Bevin, making a rare appearance in evening dress, escorting Queen Juliana and King George VI. The King, who was in high spirits that evening, had only a few more weeks to live (see p. 85).

6. Ernest Bevin addressing the ship's company, H.M.S. *Kenya*, with Capt. Brock and the author. ('Your job is to resist aggression . . . I am very worried about Korea.') (See p. 68.)

7. Ernest Bevin, whose light-weight coat is under visible strain, in the Temple Trees garden at Colombo with Mrs. Indira Gandhi, Pandit Nehru's daughter and India's future Prime Minister, and the gloomy Krishna Menon (see p. 69).

Above 8. Ernest Bevin
listens with amusement to
the guide's non-stop patter
(see p. 72).

Left 9. Ernest Bevin in the
garden at the Cairo Em-
bassy with Sir Ronald
Campbell and Prince
Philip, before going to
lunch with King Farouk
(see p. 72).

10. King Frederik, with Jean and the author at the Copenhag
Embassy, looking pleased at having just been made an Honora
Marshal of the Royal Air Force (see p. 147).

11. The Queen with the author leaving the Brussels Embassy followed
by Prince Philip and Jean (see p. 151).

12. Being received by Pope John XXIII with Harold Macmillan and Lord Home (see p. 111).

13. Herbert Morrison takes over as Foreign Secretary, full of confidence in his ability to master the job (see p. 94).

Above 14. The Duke and Duchess of Kent arriving for the Waterloo Ball at the Brussels Embassy (see p. 155).

Right 15. A second career—the author as Chairman of Barclays in France welcoming the British Ambassador, Sir Christopher Soames, at the opening of a branch in the Champs Elysées (see p. 28).

Ernie was normally quite unconcerned when acting as host to royal or other exalted guests. On one occasion when he was giving a luncheon at Carlton Gardens for Queen Juliana of the Netherlands, together with the King and Queen, the party had assembled and was having drinks before going down to the dining room. I saw Ernie in converse with Jean, who, I suppose, was the most junior lady present, when an anxious Government Hospitality official went up to him to say that all was ready and he could now escort the royal guests down to luncheon. 'All right, all right,' said Ernie. 'But can't you see I'm 'aving a nice talk with Mrs Barclay and there's no 'urry.' The only occasion when I remember him being slightly hesitant was at a luncheon in the Painted Hall at Greenwich at which he was host to the French President, Monsieur Vincent Auriol and his wife, the King and Queen and the two Princesses. The Royal and Presidential party were at the High Table on the daïs and I was sitting at the far end of one of the long tables in the main hall, when, towards the end of the meal I observed Ernie peering down the tables, and sensed that he was probably looking for me and needed help. I accordingly walked up the hall and round to the back of his chair and enquired whether there was any problem. 'I don't know 'ow we get out of 'ere,' he replied, and indeed I saw his difficulty and made some suggestions about how he should organise the departure of his distinguished guests when they got up from the table. The Queen (Queen Elizabeth, the Queen Mother) who was sitting next to him, listened with an amused smile to my suggestions, and in the event all went well. On such occasions Mrs Bevin was no help at all, though she would chatter away quite amiably to her table companions.

Ernie Bevin had a marked talent for establishing good relations with foreigners. I doubt whether there has ever been a closer or more fruitful understanding between an American Secretary of State and a British Foreign Secretary than that which existed between Dean Acheson and Ernie Bevin. The mutual confidence which, as recounted in the previous chapter, was firmly established after their first meetings in Washington in April 1949, blossomed into a firm friendship. After Ernie's death Dean wrote: 'To work with him inevitably evoked deep affection, respect, and trust. It could not be otherwise, because his indomitable courage, his simplicity and directness, his love of his country and his understanding

G

of the grandeur of its contribution to the cause of human liberty, his humanity and knowledge of the struggles and aspirations of his fellow men, his own warm affectionate good humour, made him both loved and trusted.'

The relationship with Dean Acheson was by no means an isolated case. The second most influential foreign colleague during my period as Private Secretary was undoubtedly Monsieur Schuman, and with him too Ernie Bevin was on terms of confident friendship—at least until the project for the European Coal and Steel Community was launched. Monsieur Spaak and Dr Stikker were other good and valued friends in Western Europe. Among the Commonwealth Ministers with whom he had to deal he had a specially warm relationship with Mike Pearson, who often proved a valuable ally. He even achieved the difficult task of winning the confidence both of Pandit Nehru and of Ghulam Mohammed of Pakistan.

One could not help being struck by the deference shown to Ernie by his foreign colleagues at international meetings, particularly during the last year or so of his life when it was generally known that his health was declining. Very often it seemed that a discussion was hanging fire until he elected to intervene—and he attached great importance to the timing of his statements. I would not claim that they always attained their objective—sometimes indeed they were so obscurely worded that foreign listeners in particular tended to be confused—but it was remarkable how often he succeeded in bringing life to a hitherto sterile debate. Sometimes it looked as though he was not attending, or even dozing, but he would suddenly come to life and it would become clear that he had not missed anything that had been said. There were not many, apart of course from the Russians, who risked crossing swords with him, and those who aroused his ire were sometimes pretty roughly treated.

Among the foreign Ambassadors in London I have already mentioned Lew Douglas, who had a special relationship with Ernie, but another and very different Ambassador who was a friend and admirer was the Egyptian, Amr Pasha. With the French Ambassador, Monsieur Massigli, he found it more difficult to establish a close relationship, partly because he could not understand Monsieur Massigli's English. (He was not alone in this.)

All these very different characters were impressed by Ernie's courage, integrity and steadfastness, but they were also attracted by his very human qualities. Charm does not somehow seem quite the right word for such a rugged personality, but there was something very warm about him. By all ordinary standards his was an ugly face, but when it broke into a smile it had a certain attraction and his chuckle was most endearing. Unless he was feeling unwell, in which case he could be surly and morose, looking like thunder and with his jaw working as though he was chewing the cud, he was extraordinarily good company.

I have sometimes wondered how Ernie and Dulles would have got on. I think Ernie would have found Dulles a tough nut to crack and I do not suppose he would have much liked him, but I believe he would have been more successful than Selwyn Lloyd or Anthony Eden in establishing a working relationship with him. As a rule Ernie was particularly good at dealing with Americans, at least when they met face to face. (At a distance there could be sharp differences and critical outbursts as in the sorry series of disagreements about Palestine.) When, in September 1949, he and Stafford Cripps were discussing our financial difficulties in Washington the latter's lucid and well-marshalled presentation of our case seemed to cut little ice until Ernie followed up with a more involved but perhaps more human line of argument. A touch of humour, and occasionally of sentiment, and a more earthy way of expressing himself at once brought about a change of atmosphere, and the United States Treasury proved after all to be quite sympathetic.

The ability to get on well with foreigners is a valuable asset for a Foreign Secretary, but to be a good negotiator is even more important. (Admittedly, you cannot get very far as a negotiator unless you can first inspire confidence in those with whom you have to deal.) Negotiation was an art of which Ernie Bevin had had plenty of experience, not only when confronting the employers but also within the British Trade Union Movement and in his dealings with foreign Trade Unionists. When, some thirty years previously, he had won fame as 'the Dockers' K.C.' he had shown his exceptional gift for presenting a case, combining complete mastery of the facts with the occasional unexpected flash of imagination. He had learnt the importance of studying the weaknesses of the opposition.

'When you're negotiating with Boilermakers you wants to speak very low—they're all a bit deaf' was one of his tips.

He had discovered at an early stage that if he was to achieve results by negotiation it was essential to be realistic and to recognise that an element of compromise was a necessary ingredient. (It was the reluctance of the Russians to accept this idea of compromise that made negotiations with them so difficult in the post-war years.) If required Ernie could be very persistent and he could outstay most people—even if it meant continuing the discussion into the early hours of the morning. He observed on one occasion: 'I think patience in negotiation is very essential. Somebody has to get worn out anyway.' He would doubtless have been quite prepared to face the all-night sessions which have become a feature of Common Market ministerial meetings, and would probably have judged correctly the point at which it was necessary to make concessions.

He was remarkably good at sensing the atmosphere of a meeting and at penetrating the thoughts of other participants. To give but one instance, I well remember a meeting of NATO ministers which must have taken place fairly soon after the Korean war began. The atmosphere at the outset was decidedly sticky and Dean Acheson was growing impatient with the apparently uncooperative attitude of some of his colleagues. Ernie Bevin then intervened, to say in substance: 'I know what is worrying all my European friends, though they daren't say so. They are afraid that the United States with its Pacific preoccupations is going to leave them in the lurch.' He had hit the nail on the head, and Dean, who had failed to perceive what was wrong, was then able to set some of their apprehensions at rest.

Among other gifts Ernie had an astonishing memory. He came out from time to time with quite unexpected pieces of information that he had picked up, often many years previously. He could also remember what other Ministers had said at some previous meeting, and would quote them correctly. He sometimes asked us to check whether Molotov or Vyshinsky had not made some particular statement at one of the earlier Foreign Ministers' Conferences (of which we always had the records available when negotiating with the Russians) and he was almost invariably right.

Other qualities which he possessed in high degree were vision and imagination. He had an ability to sense where danger lay, and the capacity to envisage practical ways of dealing with the problems looming ahead. He spent much time, particularly (as already mentioned) in the early hours of the morning, pondering on the foreign affairs issues of the moment, and often at our first meeting of the day he would come out with some new plan or proposition which he wished to have examined. Sometimes of course his ideas were unrealistic, but it was surprising how often they contained something of value on which to build.

I have already referred to what is often quoted as a classic example of an imaginative act on Ernie Bevin's part, his seizure of the opening offered by General Marshall's Harvard speech and the development from this of the Marshall Plan for the economic recovery of Western Europe. Up till then, as he frequently recalled in subsequent speeches, he had been seriously concerned lest the economic chaos in Western Europe should lead to a Communist takeover in France and Italy and perhaps elsewhere. He had, he used to say, at one time feared that it would only be possible to save the outer crust of Western Europe. He was not very specific about what the 'outer crust' would include, but he was presumably contemplating the loss of Western Germany as well as France and Italy.

The successful conclusion of the Atlantic Pact had provided a firm base for the defence of the West, but he saw that in spite of the prejudices which were still strong in Britain, and which to some extent he shared, the Alliance needed Western German participation in order to give it greater solidity and geographical depth. He was at the same time much concerned to help bring about a genuine reconciliation between France and Germany—in which he had a valuable ally in the person of M. Schuman. This being so it may be asked why he reacted so adversely to the 'Schuman Plan' for a European Coal and Steel Community.

One reason for his hostility was undoubtedly the feeling that the British Government had been deliberately kept in the dark and that, in spite of protestations to the contrary, the plan had been designed to exclude the United Kingdom. It made matters worse when he discovered that the Americans had been informed of the proposals before he was. He was anyhow of a suspicious nature and there was nothing he disliked more than the feeling that something had been going on behind his back of which he ought to have been informed.

It is difficult now to recapture the atmosphere of those days, and many things have become clear to us which were then much less obvious. Ernie recognised that Britain had emerged with greatly diminished power as a result of nearly five years of war, but I am not sure that he fully grasped to what an extent we had been permanently weakened. We still had a dominating position in Western Europe in 1950. The Commonwealth was still a potent force, and our 'special relationship' with the United States was very much a reality. The idea that Britain might stand to gain by abandoning her traditional policy of cheap food imports and merging her economy with those of her Western European neighbours, most of whom were still suffering to some extent from the aftermath of enemy occupation, or, in the case of Germany, from the physical destruction of the war, did not command ready acceptance. Ernie had always been a strong believer in Western European unity and had proclaimed the need for it in many speeches. He had indeed advocated an economic United States of Europe in a speech at the Trade Union Congress so long ago as 1927. But the principles which lay behind the Schuman Plan did not seem to him to be reconcilable with basic British interests. If he had been alive twenty years later and had experienced the changes in our fortunes which the next two decades have brought with them I suspect that his attitude would have been different.

Looking back at the period of Ernie Bevin's tenure of office as Foreign Secretary one cannot help being struck by the consistency with which, once he had made up his mind where British interests lay, he pursued his long-term aims. At times he was inevitably driven off course by events over which he had no control, and, as already mentioned, this was particularly the case in his handling of the problems of Palestine and the Middle East where he was frequently the victim of unexpected shifts of policy on the part of the Americans. He was, furthermore, constantly hampered by British economic and military weakness. That he was able to achieve so much at a time when our political fortunes were in reality declining all too rapidly was due in large measure to the force of his own personality and to the respect in which he was held both in Europe and in North America.

As a young man Ernie had been in demand as a preacher in Baptist and Methodist chapels in Bristol but had long since ceased to be a regular church- or chapel-goer or to take any part in institutional religion. In some respects he had moved a long way from the Nonconformist attitudes of his youth, but a good deal yet remained. Though perhaps not consciously inspired by Christian principles he had high moral standards in his approach to international affairs, and was in many ways an idealist. He hated oppression in any form and was deeply shocked by what he had seen of Communist systems. His strong dislike of Molotov and other Russian leaders was attributable in part at least to his antipathy to the régime they represented. He always accepted the need to be ready to take up arms in order to combat the forces of evil in the world. (He had bitterly opposed the pacifism of George Lansbury in the 1930s.) His first aim, however, was to serve his fellow men by establishing peace on firm foundations. Another objective was to improve the lot of the under-privileged, not only in the West but also in the less developed countries of the world. The Colombo Plan, which owed so much to his inspiration, was a practical attempt to do this for the peoples of South-East Asia. The Nile Waters agreement with Egypt of May 1949 was a source of pride because he believed that it was going to raise the standard of living of the Fellaheen. It was because he was convinced that he had a vital contribution to make towards the attainment of these objectives that he drove himself on, regardless of ill health, in his determination to achieve as much as was humanly possible before being finally compelled to give way to another.

Ernie's physical disabilities made those who were close to him want to protect him from all unnecessary strain and effort, but there was a limit to what was possible, for he insisted on knowing all that was going on. One of the few occasions on which I received a reprimand, albeit a gentle one, was when I deliberately did not ring him up in hospital to tell him the moment I heard that hostilities had begun in Korea. If he thought it was his duty to accept some new commitment it was very difficult to dissuade him. I have referred to his determination to make the trip to Ceylon for the Colombo Conference, but it is perhaps worth expanding on this. In the period immediately before our departure he was far from well, and Alec McCall insisted on obtaining the opinion of eminent medical colleagues to establish whether they agreed with his conclusion that the Secretary of State was not fit to undertake the journey. They were unanimous that he ought not to go. But Ernie believed, doubtless rightly, that if he did not go to the Conference little would be achieved. He therefore turned to Alec and said that he had made up his mind to go, but he would be very grateful if Alec would accompany him. In the circumstances Alec felt unable to refuse, though it meant deserting his other patients for a whole month.

Ernie recognised that he was something of a prima donna but he seemed to feel that this was his right. He is reputed to have said of himself 'I'm a turn-up in a million.' If he did, this was if anything an understatement for he was surely unique. He was undoubtedly vain and egotistical but in such an unabashed way that I at least was always ready to excuse him and was amused rather than irritated. He sometimes resented public criticism but it did not deflect him from his purpose. He enjoyed applause but not flattery. I certainly never thought of expressing admiration or approval unless I genuinely felt that it was due.

Accounts of Ernie Bevin in his earlier days tend to stress his pugnacity, his vindictiveness and the harsher sides of his character. He was described as 'a good hater'. There was certainly nothing soft about him but by the time I went to work with him he had greatly mellowed. He was still a tough antagonist, conscious of his power and confident of his ability to deal with any opposition, but I fancy that in his early days at the Foreign Office he was more combative and more obstreperous than in my time. He could still be difficult, suspicious and moody, but advancing years and his physical disabilities had, I think, tended to make him less ruthless and more tolerant.

It will have emerged clearly enough from what I have already said about Ernie's character and his personality that I for one was his devoted admirer. In a tribute to him shortly after his death Attlee singled out as one of his outstanding qualities the ability to inspire affection in all those who worked for him. With this I fully agree, and the closer one was to him the more potent was the spell. I have never felt the same degree of personal devotion, combined with affection, for any other individual for whom or with whom I have worked.

There was something boyish about Ernie which was very disarming. He had a strong sense of humour and loved to laugh or to make others laugh at his stories. As will have appeared from previous chapters, he thoroughly enjoyed a good party. He was quite undisciplined, notably over what he ate and drank. Alec McCall used to try to persuade him to stick either to whisky or to champagne in the course of one evening, but he seldom did. He knew when he was disobeying the rules and ruefully admitted afterwards that he had been unwise. As he put it to Alec soon after the latter took him on, 'I know, if I do your don'ts I'm in trouble.'

Before I had been with Ernie for many weeks I began to feel confident that our relationship would be a success. This may sound complacent, but I believe that he found my presence reassuring. I was a calming influence when this was needed and a simplifier rather than a complicator. He certainly seemed to like to tell me all that was on his mind and before long I knew just what he thought about all those with whom we had to deal.

The two years which I spent with him were a strenuous and exhausting period. The programme was always exacting and neither in London nor at Conferences abroad did one have quite enough time to get through all that had to be done. It was only on our journeys that there were opportunities to relax. But I never for one moment regretted that I had been given the chance to work so closely with this extraordinary man. I never ceased to be fascinated, and in his company one could never be dull.

From time to time he would say something to show that he was appreciative of what I was able to do for him. On more than one occasion he said to me, 'I would like to make you a Sir', and I had to assure him that I was much too junior and that this was quite out of the question. Anyhow I felt amply rewarded by his friendship and confidence and by the knowledge that I was serving a Secretary of State the like of whom we should never see again. I continue to think that I am extremely fortunate to have had the experience of working with him during the last two years of his life.

5

HERBERT MORRISON—FOREIGN SECRETARY

HERBERT MORRISON'S appointment as Secretary of State for Foreign Affairs was announced on 9 March 1951 and he was to remain at the Foreign Office until the fall of the Labour Government after the election in late October of that year. This relatively short period amply sufficed to show up his inadequacy for the job, and it would probably be agreed that he was the worst British Foreign Secretary since Sir John Simon. His failure was the more surprising since his previous political career had been one of almost unbroken success. At the Ministries of Transport and Supply, the Home Office, the Ministry of Home Security, and finally as Lord President of the Council and Deputy Prime Minister he had won general acclaim as an effective and decisive Minister. His appointment to the Foreign Office was welcomed by much of the Press and most people at that time thought that he should do well there. The Foreign Office itself had been sad to see Ernie Bevin go, but it had been assumed for some time that his retirement could not be long delayed, and though it had been known that Ernie disliked and mistrusted Morrison I do not think this attitude was shared by his officials or that there was any sort of prejudice against Morrison. Indeed, in some ways it was a relief that we could now look to having a fit and active Foreign Secretary (Morrison was then sixty-three) in place of an ageing invalid.

I was destined to be Morrison's Principal Private Secretary for all but the last three weeks of his term of office so I was well placed to observe why the expectations aroused by his appointment were not fulfilled.

In accordance with the normal practice, Morrison took over all the existing staff of the Private Office. My assistants and I realised from the outset that we were about to experience a considerable change in the established pattern, but the previous contacts I had

had with our new chief had left quite a favourable impression and I think I can claim that we were all prepared to welcome him and to adjust ourselves as necessary to the new régime.

One slight complication appeared at the outset in the person of Miss Donald, a lady who had worked for Morrison for many years in his various previous offices and who was to remain across the road at No. 11 Downing Street where she had operated while he was Lord President. She had become a close friend and confidante and was a stout defender of what she supposed to be her master's interests, but official Foreign Office commitments came low in her order of priorities and she was constantly making plans which clashed with engagements made for the Secretary of State in the Private Office. One way and another she did not help to smooth the way for the new Foreign Secretary.

Mrs Morrison played little part in our affairs. She occasionally made a reluctant appearance at some official function, but much preferred to remain at home at Eltham. She had had no desire to move into the official Foreign Secretary's flat at 1 Carlton Gardens so there was no problem about the Bevins staying on there. Her health was giving cause for anxiety, and (as I subsequently learnt) the Secretary of State was told by her doctors only a few weeks after his arrival at the Foreign Office that she was suffering from cancer. As I have indicated in a previous chapter Flo Bevin had her faults, but at least she was warm-hearted and cheerful and provided a sort of home life which was almost totally lacking for poor Morrison.

Meanwhile first impressions in the Office were not altogether encouraging. Our attempts to help by explaining some of the peculiarities of the Foreign Office system did not seem to be too welcome and were apt to be met by hints that he would soon change all that. He made it clear that in his view a great gulf was fixed between Ministers and officials. Whereas Ernie had called all the members of his Private Office, and indeed most of the senior members of the Foreign Office, by their Christian names and had treated us very much as members of the family, Herbert Morrison preferred to keep his distance, and throughout the seven months I was with him I was always addressed as Barclay. In his autobiography he comments on the 'easy-going familiarity' with which the Foreign Office officials treated each other, which was apparently quite unlike what he had been used to in the Home Office. 'Even Secretaries of State,' he observed, 'have been known to address Foreign Office civil servants by their Christian names.' It looks as though this practice quite shocked him! If so he is the only post-war Foreign Secretary to have adopted this rather old-fashioned attitude.

One unexpected complication was Morrison's extraordinary ignorance of most of the Foreign Office problems of the moment. He had wanted to be Foreign Secretary in 1945 and it was commonly believed that he had for long been pressing his claims to succeed Ernie Bevin, so that there was no question of the appointment having come as a surprise to him. Moreover, as a senior Cabinet Minister for the past ten years, with only one short gap, he had been supplied with all important Foreign Office telegrams and despatches, and had every opportunity to keep himself informed. He seemed to lack not only the background knowledge but also the ability to comprehend the essentials of the problems before him. It was not long before this became apparent both to his colleagues in the Cabinet and to Parliament—with disastrous results.

Our new chief seemed to be appalled by the amount of work he was expected to do. He had apparently been under the illusion that the Foreign Office was like any other Government Department and that with proper organisation it should not be necessary for him to work long or erratic hours. He particularly resented the nightly 'Box' and asked me to try to reduce the volume of reading material that went into it. This was just not possible if he was going to do the job properly, as I did not fail to point out. From time to time he made suggestions for shedding some of his work on to the junior Ministers, but so long as the Foreign Secretary remains answerable for all that is done in his name it is difficult to go very far in the direction of sharing out the load. Morrison did not seem to have anticipated the constant need for urgent decisions. Particularly in the early days we would find that papers recommending some specific course of action, or perhaps setting out two or more alternatives, would return with a critical comment or query in the margin but no indication of what he wanted done. All this made life for the Private Secretary frustrating and complicated.

One of the basic reasons for Morrison's failure as Foreign

Secretary was his preoccupation with internal politics. This was not entirely Morrison's own fault for very soon after his arrival at the Foreign Office Attlee went into hospital, and for the next few weeks Morrison had to act as Prime Minister. Moreover this was the period of the dispute over health charges which led finally to the resignation of Bevan and Wilson, and Morrison could hardly help becoming deeply involved.

Another counter-attraction which kept Morrison away from dealing with foreign affairs was the Festival of Britain. This had been very much his brain-child so that he was naturally anxious to do all he could to ensure its success and was determined to participate in all the opening ceremonies. But he unwisely gave the impression that the Festival took priority over Foreign Office business, which he was prepared to leave in the hands of the Minister of State, Kenneth Younger, and the Parliamentary Under Secretaries.

Morrison often left his junior Ministers to answer Foreign Office questions in the House and when he did speak he contrived to give the impression that he was uncertain of his facts—which was often all too true. His parliamentary reputation, which in his previous posts had been high, suffered a major blow from a particularly ineffective winding-up speech in a debate on Persia at the end of June. He quite failed to give any clear picture of the policy the Government were following and was sharply attacked not only by the Opposition but by much of the Press.

A minor incident, which Morrison took all too seriously, arose as a result of his sensitivity about his pronunciation of foreign names. He liked to have a phonetic rendering in the margin of his notes when making a speech, and this was normally provided, but unfortunately we assumed that he would know how to pronounce the rivers Tigris and Euphrates. He did not, and when he put the accent on the wrong syllable in both a titter went round the House. To make matters worse Winston mischievously pretended that he had not quite heard the name of the second river and asked for it to be repeated. I was sitting in the officials' box in the House at the time and realised that there was trouble ahead.

Morrison's parliamentary setbacks were the more galling to him in that, unlike Ernie Bevin, he was a devoted House of Commons man. There were of course disadvantages in Ernie's relative remoteness from Parliament and there is no doubt that Morrison found it relaxing to go and pass the evening in the House, chatting to colleagues and sensing the mood. But it seemed to me at the time that he could ill afford to spend so many hours in this way when he was simultaneously complaining about the volume of Foreign Office work and the number of papers he was expected to read.

It was difficult to give good service to a Secretary of State who had so many other preoccupations and for whom—in contrast to Ernie Bevin or Anthony Eden—the Foreign Office did not seem to have absolute priority. He for his part probably felt that he did not get the help and support from his officials that he had had from his small côterie, led by Max Nicholson, at the Lord President's office. He seemed to take a long time to realise how different the two jobs were and how impossible it was to be an effective Foreign Secretary unless he devoted himself almost exclusively to this most exacting of posts.

By far the most difficult issue with which Morrison was confronted during his period of office was the Anglo-Iranian oil dispute. This had come to a head at the end of April as a result of the nationalisation of the assets of the Anglo-Iranian Oil Co. by the extreme right-wing Government of Dr Mossadeq. It is not necessary here to recount the sequence of events during the months that followed. The main point is that the British Government, in the person of the Foreign Secretary, gave the impression that they had no consistent policy and that they were alternately dominated by the views of the hawks and the doves in the Cabinet. At the outset Morrison was undoubtedly a hawk. He had earlier let it be known that of his many predecessors the one he admired most was Palmerston and this dispute seemed at first an occasion for Palmerstonian methods. It has to be remembered that Britain's position in the world was very much stronger then than now and we had not learnt the bitter lesson of Suez that military intervention is no longer possible without the support of very powerful friends. At various stages, then, Morrison seemed to be threatening the use of force but each time he drew back and was then exposed to Opposition complaints that he was preparing to 'scuttle'. He was also accused of failing to take adequate steps to protect British lives and property. His position was undoubtedly a very difficult one and his freedom of movement was limited by the opposition of Attlee and of the majority of his Cabinet colleagues to direct military intervention. American pressure, too, was constantly exerted in favour of a negotiated settlement, and the public attitude adopted by some of the American officials involved was by no means helpful.

During the latter part of August Morrison was on holiday and went on a cruise to the Norwegian fiords. At the end of the month the situation in the Middle East was so acute that the Foreign Office sent him a telegram advising him to return. He refused point blank, maintaining that he needed more of a break. Perhaps he did, but the message was not sent lightly and his reaction created a very unfavourable impression.

Morrison's policies on the other main issues that confronted him during the spring and summer of 1951 tended in general to follow the lines set by his predecessor. He was as anti-Communist as Ernie had been. On European questions there was little difference between them. Like Ernie, Morrison was unenthusiastic about the Council of Europe, though as a result of a visit to Strasbourg in August he was latterly rather less inclined to criticise its activities. I do not think it ever occurred to him that the United Kingdom might one day seek to play a more active part in European integration. For him the Schuman Plan was definitely a matter for the Continentals. He wished them well but remained basically detached. He was perhaps slightly more sympathetic to the Germans than Ernie had been and he fully accepted the need for German rearmament.

Our relations with the Arab world, and in particular Egypt, continued to give us much trouble and the arguments about the British position in the Canal Zone and the future of the Sudan continued throughout the summer. The Korean war on the other hand had moved into a less critical stage and no longer presented the same political complications.

A totally different but very disagreeable problem with which Herbert Morrison found himself saddled, rather unluckily, was the Burgess and Maclean affair. On the whole he dealt with it in a sensible and practical manner and I do not think it disturbed him as much as it would have done Ernie Bevin or Anthony Eden, who both felt themselves much more closely identified with the well-being of the Foreign Service than did Morrison. When I was first

informed by the head of the Foreign Office Security Department
of the evidence against Maclean, I found it scarcely credible. However, it soon became necessary to inform the Secretary of State and
to get his approval for the steps contemplated by the Security
authorities, including an early confrontation with Maclean. He
readily agreed, and this was to have taken place towards the end
of May, but as is well known, the two were tipped off, presumably
by Philby, and made a hurried getaway just in time to escape from
the net which was beginning to close round them.

For the Foreign Office as a whole the Burgess and Maclean
affair was a shattering blow. As I knew both individuals it is perhaps worth taking another look at the sordid story.

It was not always realised how different the two cases were.
Burgess had been imported into the Foreign Office by Hector
McNeil, then Minister of State, who wanted to have him in his
Private Office to help with speech writing and so on. It sounded
reasonable enough, particularly in view of Burgess' very distinguished academic record as a scholar of Trinity, Cambridge. He
had many eminent friends—including for example Harold Nicolson—and no shortage of sponsors. Needless to say no one came
forward to warn the Foreign Office Personnel Department that his
private life was disreputable or that his political views were far to
the left of Hector McNeil's. All the same he did not make a favourable impression and the Department successfully resisted pressure
from Hector, who anyway soon found him less useful than he had
hoped, to get him established in the senior branch of the Service.
He was ultimately admitted to what was then called Branch B, the
executive and clerical grade, and after an unsuccessful spell in a
Foreign Office department was appointed to the Embassy in Washington. Here he proved a disastrous liability and was on the point
of being dismissed from the Service when he defected. Though the
many lurid stories about his past which have since been revealed
were unknown to the Foreign Office at that time, Burgess had
never been regarded as a useful member of society, and the shock
of finding that he had all along been a spy was not quite so shattering as the discovery about Maclean.

Maclean came from a highly respectable and distinguished
Liberal family, had had a very good academic record and had
passed the exacting pre-war Diplomatic Service examination. He

had done well in a number of posts and his office work was of a high class. He had worked under me in Paris in 1940 and we had subsequently overlapped for a short time in Washington. There he had been my under-study on the Anglo-American committee charged with working out peace terms for Italy, and he had made a considerable impression by his skill at drafting and his ability to unravel highly complex issues. Though he appeared shy and withdrawn and did not mix freely I for one never saw him drunk or disorderly. I believe this became much more common at a later stage and notably when he went to Cairo. The reports that then reached Personnel Department (I had left it by that time) gave a very watered down version of what had been going on, though even so they were enough to cause his recall to London for psychiatric treatment.

After the two spies had fled many people expressed astonishment that the Foreign Office was so ill-informed about the disreputable private lives of the two men. But the trouble was that those who were in the know, whether members of the Service or not, did not then think it their duty to tell the authorities concerned what was going on. The most astonishing admission has been that of a well-known writer who was clearly informed by Burgess himself that he was a Russian spy but took no action until it was too late. So far as the Service itself is concerned the instructions about reporting on staff and the investigation of personal weaknesses and ideologies were promptly made much more stringent. Before Maclean it had seemed inconceivable that a regular member of the Service could be a Russian spy. Now, unfortunately, nothing can be excluded.

Understandably enough the Foreign Office suffered severely at the hands of the Press but I do not think the affair had any great effect on Morrison's reputation. His responsibility for what had happened was clearly limited and in the eyes of the public he was not equated with the Foreign Office in the way that Ernie would have been.

Turning again to Morrison's conduct of foreign policy, it is only fair to point out, in extenuation of the lack of direction or of positive initiative which characterised his time at the Foreign Office, that in 1951 the Attlee Government, with its very slender majority in the House of Commons, was in a weak position. It was, more-

H

over, suffering from the loss of its two outstanding personalities, Bevin and Cripps, and to a lesser extent from the resignation of Bevan. The fact remains that Morrison failed not only to win the confidence of the House of Commons but even that of his own collegeaues in the Government. This must have been primarily due to their realisation of his basic lack of understanding of the problems he put before them. Even when he had a good case and a clear brief from the Foreign Office it seems that he failed to carry conviction. As a result other members of the Cabinet began to think that they knew as much about Foreign Affairs as he did and there was a surprising occasion when Stokes, then Minister of Works, put round a paper setting out his own ideas about what our policy towards Egypt should be. In Ernie's day it would have been unthinkable for a colleague to trespass on his domain in such a way.

As I have already recounted, foreign trips with Ernie, though exhausting and sometimes harassing on account of his health, were nearly always fascinating experiences. He could be relied on to do and say the right thing whether calling on foreign Heads of State, or meeting with NATO chiefs, or American Trade Unionists, or Asian Commonwealth politicians. Herbert Morrison on the other hand had little gift for establishing good relations with foreigners, whether statesmen or others, and I never felt confident about how he would behave.

Our first two outings were to Paris, but I have no clear recollection of how we fared. On the other hand I remember very vividly our visit to Vienna in May 1951. This ought to have been a straightforward and agreeable trip for all concerned, for the Austrians are excellent hosts and were keen to make a success of the first visit of a British Foreign Secretary to their country since the war. Indeed, I believe it was the first since the Congress of Vienna. Unfortunately one of Morrison's theories was that it should be possible for the Foreign Secretary, even when on an official visit, to discard his ministerial status and behave like an ordinary tourist. In accordance with this doctrine he had arranged that on the night on which the Austrian Government were giving an official dinner in his honour, Miss Donald should come and pick him up at 10 p.m. at the Hofburg, and they would then go off on a round of night haunts. I told them both that the Austrians would be very hurt if he left their party at such an early hour, and they would not be favourably impressed when they learnt, as they certainly would, why he had disappeared and where he had spent the rest of the evening. Moreover he might well find that the official party was quite a good one. I was told in effect that I was a stuffy Foreign Office official and that I was not to try to sabotage this plan. In the event I won my point, for as I had prophesied, the Austrian party was gay and cheerful, being enlivened by singers and musicians from the Vienna Opera, and at 10 o'clock Morrison accepted that he could not possibly walk out. I went down to the entrance hall to tell a very angry lady that the Secretary of State could not join her and that she had better go home.

Our other evening in Vienna was also not without incident. Our High Commissioner, Harold Caccia, had arranged a dinner party to enable Morrison to meet a number of prominent Austrian politicians, Provincial Governors, Trade Union leaders and the like, for all of whom the visit of the British Foreign Secretary was a great occasion. They naturally looked forward to discussing their country's problems with their distinguished visitor at or after dinner. Our Herbert however had different ideas and as soon as dinner was over he suggested to Nancy Caccia that the carpet should be rolled back and music provided for dancing. Looking round at the middle-aged if not elderly Austrians present and at their none too sprightly wives it did not seem a very auspicious occasion for a dance, and anyhow this was not at all the object of the evening. Nancy was not amused and made this quite clear before Harold finally vetoed the suggestion and made poor Morrison get down to talking about the problems of the Occupation. By backing up our host and hostess I had again appeared in the rôle of a spoil-sport.

My next visit to Vienna with a British Minister was ten years later when I went there with Ted Heath. This was a very different affair. We had Johannes Schwarzenberg, then Austrian Ambassador in London, in attendance and enjoyed a guided tour of the Schwarzenberg Palais as well as of the great Vienna picture gallery and the Lippizaners' stables. But one of the highlights occurred when, having obtained access to the organ loft of the cathedral, the Stefansdom, Ted Heath sat down and began to play, to the astonishment of the Austrians present.

But to return to Herbert Morrison, a trip to Bonn, which in fact preceded that to Vienna, had passed off well enough. We stayed, in great comfort but away from the temptations of the city, at the palatial Schloss Röttgen, then the residence of the High Commissioner, Ivone Kirkpatrick and his wife. The official talks with Dr Adenauer were rather successful and the latter publicly expressed his warm satisfaction at the improvement in Anglo-German relations.

On 6 September we set off for San Francisco for the signing of the Japanese Peace Treaty. We should have gone sooner had Morrison not delayed his return from Norway and Kenneth Younger had to be despatched in advance to speak at the opening ceremony. We flew first to New York, passing over Greenland, and then on across the continent. In those days it was a long and tiring trip. San Francisco is always a pleasant city, and this should have been a great occasion, but our visit was too short and somehow the arrangements for the actual signature did not seem to do justice to the historic character of the occasion. We flew back to Washington with Dean Acheson in the special plane of the American delegation, and quite a lot of business was transacted en route. The subsequent discussions at the State Department were uninspired and colourless affairs compared to some of the Bevin–Acheson sessions I had attended.

From Washington we flew on to a meeting of the Atlantic Council in Ottawa, where we were met by Gaitskell and Shinwell. The main subjects of discussion were the future status of West Germany and the sharing of Occupation costs. Morrison was not impressive. 'He could be counted on to deepen the gloom that surrounded our talks,' was Acheson's comment. He added that 'Morrison's unfortunate manner constantly rasped our patience.'*

On the Sunday the Secretary of State and his party were invited to spend the day at a lake to the north of Ottawa. After lunch Morrison said he would like to go for a swim, while I had organised a fishing expedition for myself. I was out in a boat and had caught several bass on a trout fly when I became aware of a commotion near the shore. It emerged that poor Herbert, who was a very moderate swimmer, breast-stroke only, had ventured out too far and got into real trouble. He only saved himself by clinging to a semi-submerged rock until anxious helpers came and rescued him.

* D. Acheson, *Present at the Creation* (London, 1969).

He was fairly badly scratched but otherwise none the worse. My fishing was cut short and I had to accompany a very irritable Secretary of State back to the Château Laurier Hotel.

It was while we were in Ottawa that Attlee announced the date of the General Election. Morrison did not agree with the decision and complained that he had not been consulted. In actual fact we had received a personal message from No. 10 which was meant to alert him to what was proposed but it was couched in rather cryptic terms and Morrison failed to spot its significance. In passing it to him I naturally assumed that he knew what it was all about while he was presumably reluctant to admit that he had no idea what it meant.

We sailed for home from New York in the *Queen Mary*, getting back at the very end of September. A few days later I was to hand over my responsibilities as Private Secretary to Evelyn Shuckburgh.

As the time of my release drew near the prospect of a change became increasingly attractive. I was being promoted to be an Under Secretary, but as I well knew, the post was much less arduous than that of Private Secretary, and after two and a half years I was not sorry to have a slight let-up. I duly received a very nicely worded letter of thanks from the Secretary of State, but the effect was rather spoilt by my knowing that none of it was his own handiwork. Owing to a slip up by one of our girls I had seen the draft which had been prepared by Freddie Leishman, my assistant. Not a comma was changed in the final version. Morrison and I parted with mutual expressions of goodwill, but I had no feelings of regret. It had been very different when I saw Ernie off from the Park door of the Foreign Office for the last time.

I like to think that I made a success of my personal relations with Ernie, whereas I have to admit that with Morrison I failed. My previous experience as Private Secretary ought to have been helpful to him but perhaps after all he would have done better to have made a change and taken on someone who had not been so close to his predecessor. Not that I think that any other Private Secretary could have enabled Morrison to make a success of his job as Foreign Secretary. Dean Acheson summed him up as 'a friend of many qualities and abilities but none fitting him to deal with foreign affairs or foreigners'. It is surprising all the same that a man of such undoubted political talents should have made quite such a hash of the job. I have endeavoured to suggest some of the reasons but perhaps there was one other—that although only sixty-three his powers were beginning to decline.

The defeat of the Labour Party in the election on 25 October meant that Morrison's departure quickly followed my own. I suspect that he himself was relieved to be leaving a post where he had so signally failed to distinguish himself and where he had never really felt at home. To quote Acheson once more, 'his departure [was] as welcome to him as to others'.

Morrison doubtless realised that his spell at the Foreign Office had done no good to his political career and to his prospects of becoming Prime Minister. Nevertheless he remained the heir-apparent for the party leadership and until 1955 it was generally assumed that when Attlee finally retired Morrison would succeed him. In the event, of course, the prize eluded him and though Attlee's determination to stay on as long as possible was the prime reason for Morrison's ultimate discomfiture his failure at the Foreign Office no doubt played a part.

6

OTHER BRITISH FOREIGN SECRETARIES AND A FEW FOREIGN MINISTERS

I SERVED ALTOGETHER under eleven British Foreign Secretaries, though with some of them I had little direct contact. This was certainly true of the first two, Sir John Simon and Sir Samuel Hoare, neither of whom won many laurels during their period at the Foreign Office. The former, incidentally, is an excellent example to support Lord Gladwyn's proposition that brilliant lawyers always make bad Foreign Secretaries.

Before going further I should perhaps say that, to my mind, the old adage of *de mortuis* . . . is not altogether appropriate for a chapter like this. Reasonable criticism of the dead seems to me to be quite legitimate, but a measure of restraint is called for in writing about those who are still living—particularly when they happen to have been one's political chief. Accordingly, though critical comment is by no means excluded from what follows, any reader hoping to find scandalous revelations about former Foreign Secretaries who are still with us may be disappointed.

When Sam Hoare, incidentally a distant relation of mine, was obliged to resign after the fiasco of the so-called Hoare–Laval Plan, he made way for the rising star, Anthony Eden, who for more than twenty years was to play a key rôle in foreign affairs, whether in or out of office. Like most members of the Foreign Office I was his warm admirer in the pre-war years, and in the drab and ageing Chamberlain Government he certainly stood out as a man of courage and principle. When his disagreements with Neville Chamberlain finally led to his resignation in February 1938, his action seemed to me quite right and indeed almost inescapable, but I never regarded him with the sort of hero-worship of Oliver Harvey and other of my colleagues, which caused them to view his departure from the Office as a major tragedy. When he returned to the Foreign Office in 1941 we were all delighted to see him back, and in his many disagreements with Churchill, notably over the problems of de Gaulle and the Free French, with which in a humble capacity I was then involved in Washington, I was myself invariably on Eden's side. But though I saw him on his various visits to Washington and occasionally in the Foreign Office after my return in 1944, I had relatively few personal dealings with him before the Conservatives were swept out of office by the General Election the following year.

My period as Private Secretary had come to an end shortly before Eden's return to the Foreign Office in 1951, and this was probably just as well, as I do not think I should have been well equipped to look after him during the period that followed. His experience and mastery of the technique of foreign affairs were of course exceptional and at times they enabled him to dominate an international gathering—for example the Geneva Conference on South-East Asia in 1954. But his impatience and irritability, partly no doubt due to ill-health, tended to make life very difficult for his closest associates during the next few years. Though I was usually able to calm and soothe Ernie, when this was necessary, I question whether I should have been successful with Anthony.

By the time the Suez crisis came to a head I had already left London for Copenhagen, and anyhow, having as Chief Clerk been concerned primarily with personnel and administration problems I had not been personally involved during the earlier stages of the trouble. Like most of my Foreign Office friends, all but a very small number of whom had been kept completely in the dark about what was going on, as indeed had our Ambassador in Cairo, Humphrey Trevelyan, I was astonished to see such experienced leaders embark on this adventure with such inadequate diplomatic preparation. In particular I was shocked by the failure of our communications with the Americans—something which could surely never have happened in Ernie Bevin's day, though admittedly he did not have a Dulles to deal with. I am ready to concede that there were moments during the long-drawn-out crisis when swift and decisive use of force, though of doubtful morality, might conceivably have averted more serious trouble later; but we were not organised for this and of course as things turned out we got the worst of all possible worlds. Suez was certainly a very significant milestone in the post-war decline of our political and military fortunes. It also afforded clear proof that it was no longer possible for Britain to act independently in a major crisis unless she had the backing of at least one of the World Powers. This however is clearly too big a subject to discuss in this small volume.

My first dealings with Lord Halifax as Foreign Secretary were in connection with the State Visit to London of President and Madame Lebrun in 1938. As already mentioned, I then occupied what would now be called the French Desk in the Foreign Office, and as my superiors were increasingly preoccupied with the German situation I had to a large extent to act on my own in matters relating to the State Visit. One of my concerns was with the evening entertainment at which the Foreign Secretary was host to a large and distinguished company in the old enclosed courtyard of the India Office. Arrayed in uniform and white knee breeches, I acted as one of the ushers. The programme for the evening had largely been devised by Vansittart and the theatrical items were an odd mixture, ranging from scenes from *Romeo and Juliet* to sketches by Sacha Guitry and Yvonne Printemps, but the arrangements as a whole went well and I received a note of appreciation from Lord Halifax.

I was destined to see a lot more of Lord Halifax as a result of my appointment to the Washington Embassy in April 1941. The staff of the Embassy was already large when I got there, and after Pearl Harbour it was further expanded and supplemented by numerous special missions—food, raw materials, shipping, etc.— so that Lord Halifax's empire was an extensive one and he could not be expected to have very close dealings with relatively junior members of his staff. Furthermore, his character, and probably his experience as Viceroy, tended to make him rather more aloof and remote than a career Ambassador would have thought proper or natural. Accordingly, except when acting temporarily as Head of Chancery or in occasional sudden crises, usually related to the activities of General de Gaulle, I did not have a great deal of direct contact with him in the office.

One way to get to know my Ambassador a little better was offered by his enjoyment of a game of tennis in the evenings after work, and I was often asked to help make up a four. He was a steady player and of course had the advantage of a great reach, but the most curious feature of his play was his service. Owing to his defective left arm he threw the ball up with his right hand and if the first serve was a fault he dived down to pick up the second ball which he kept at his feet. It was a long way to go and always seemed a laborious system.

Lord Halifax's appointment to Washington had been due at least in part to Winston's desire to move him out of the Foreign Office—which was not a good reason for sending him to what was then by far our most important diplomatic post. On the face of it he did not appear to be ideally qualified to establish the sort of relations which we then needed to have with the American Administration, let alone to get himself accepted by the American public. In the event his moral and intellectual qualities enabled him speedily to build up an excellent relationship with the President and with other leading figures of the Administration, notably the very influential Harry Hopkins. The arrangement whereby he remained a member of the Cabinet in London undoubtedly helped and I doubt whether any career Ambassador would have succeeded in winning for himself the freedom of communication with the White House which Lord Halifax quite soon achieved.

It was a more difficult task to win the sympathy of the great American public. This rather aloof and awe-inspiring aristocrat was not the type of Englishman who is immediately understood and welcomed in the Middle or Far West, and at any time before Pearl Harbour he was apt to be received with suspicion if not hostility. His every activity was watched with a critical eye and it was perhaps predictable, though it seemed at the time rather bad luck, that he should get a bad Press for taking one day off and indulging in his favourite pastime by going hunting in Virginia. (I was glad that I could sneak off for a very occasional day's shooting without anyone paying any attention.) Lord Halifax took great trouble, however, to visit all parts of the country for speaking or other engagements and gradually succeeded in becoming a well-known and accepted figure. The warm-hearted American public became much readier to give him a friendly hearing when they learned that he had had one son killed and another severely wounded in North Africa.

When he finally left Washington there could be no doubt at all that he had rendered great services to Anglo-American relations and it is arguable that he had proved more successful as an Ambassador than he had been as Foreign Secretary.

Harold Macmillan was only Foreign Secretary for a few months, but nevertheless he made quite an impact at the Foreign Office. I was then Chief Clerk, and he acquired merit in my eyes by taking a keen and sympathetic interest in the personnel and administration questions for which I was responsible. Soon after his appointment I was invited to go down to Birch Grove for the day to tell him what was going on within my field. As a result of his wartime appointments as Minister Resident in North Africa and in Italy he knew quite a bit about our problems and about individual members of the Service. We had an interesting and stimulating discussion in the library, while outside on the lawn Lady Dorothy was playing cricket with her grandchildren. It came as a disappointment to quite a few people in the Foreign Office when Harold Macmillan was shortly transferred to the Treasury.

Later on, when he was Prime Minister, I was to accompany him and Alec Douglas-Home on trips to Bonn and Rome. I believe that the talks in Bonn played quite an important part in convincing our two Ministers that the prospects of a successful negotiation for our entry into the Common Market were reasonably promising. Like a good many other people they over-estimated the value of German support on this issue, and failed to foresee that it would crumble when confronted with tough opposition from the French.

In the special aircraft en route for Rome I was glad to see the Prime Minister living up to his reputation by calmly reading his Trollope while the rest of us were engaged in studying our briefs or talking over the problems which were expected to arise with the Italians. At a later stage during the flight we had an interesting discussion on the theory and practice of shooting high pheasants.

While in Rome I accompanied our Ministers on a visit to the Pope, John XXIII, and was much struck by the warmth of his personality. He bustled about talking cheerfully to every member of the British contingent, and gave us each a silver coin bearing his effigy. There was an awkward moment when he thought he had not enough to go round, but an extra coin was somehow produced and he beamed contentedly on the assembled party.

I must now go back a few years to the appointment of Selwyn Lloyd to succeed Harold Macmillan at the Foreign Office. During most of his tenure of office I was in Copenhagen, so that my direct dealings with him were rather limited. He did, however, stay with us there twice, once when he accompanied the Queen on her State Visit to Denmark and on another occasion when he came for a NATO meeting. He was a very amenable and welcome guest, and I think he enjoyed both visits.

When I returned to the Foreign Office in April 1960 Alec Douglas-Home had taken over as Foreign Secretary, but in my new job dealing with European economic problems I found myself before long answerable primarily to Ted Heath, by then Lord Privy Seal. I always regretted that I did not have more direct contact with Alec, for, apart from the fact that we had mutual friends and interests in common, he is, I think, after Ernie Bevin, the Foreign Secretary for whom I would have felt best qualified to serve as Private Secretary. Whether he would have wanted me is, of course, another matter!

During the next three years I was destined to see a great deal of Ted Heath and he of me. During the period preceding the opening of negotiations in Brussels I accompanied him to various EFTA ministerial meetings and on other trips abroad, including visits to Cyprus, Athens, Vienna and Copenhagen. He handled the redoubtable Archbishop Makarios as effectively as he did the EFTA Ministers, some of whom at this period were deeply suspicious of British intentions. I soon became a warm admirer, and at some stage, though I think this was not until after the Brussels negotiations had begun in 1961, I prophesied to my family that he would one day be Prime Minister.

In the Brussels negotiations themselves Ted Heath made a notable impression, both on his own high-powered Delegation and on the various European Ministers with whom he had to deal. The fact that, in spite of ministerial differences of opinion at home, which inevitably slowed us down, we were within measurable distance of success when we finally encountered the de Gaulle veto, was due in no small part to his determination and drive. It is at any rate safe to say that no other Minister at that time could have achieved more than he did. He quickly made himself a master of all the intricate subjects with which we were involved, and none of the Ministers of the Six could equal his knowledge. There were, of course, sometimes differences of opinion within the Delegation on the tactics which we should follow, but all its members had a very high regard for our chief. On the purely personal level I can look back on numerous enjoyable occasions together in Brussels restaurants and elsewhere, though I must confess that I found it less easy to be completely relaxed with Ted than with some other political chiefs.

Of Rab Butler as Foreign Secretary I have little to say. I had known him on and off since the time when he was Parliamentary Under Secretary at the Foreign Office before the war, and was glad to welcome him when he came to stay with us in Brussels fairly soon after we got there. I nevertheless got the impression that he had slightly lost interest in foreign affairs, and it was not long before he moved on to other things. Incidentally, *The Art of the Possible** must surely be one of the best political autobiographies of recent years. Among its other merits is its relative brevity.

Most of my period in Brussels coincided with the period of Harold Wilson's administration, and Patrick Gordon-Walker's brief tenure at the Foreign Office having come to a premature close we had many visits from his two successors, Michael Stewart and George Brown. Michael Stewart's first trip abroad after taking over at the Foreign Office was to Brussels, where he came to speak at the British Chamber of Commerce Banquet, and neither he nor I knew quite what to expect. He had been provided by the Foreign Office with a draft speech which was much too long and too serious, but he made the best of it, and, on the following day, when we had a session with Monsieur Spaak, Michael Stewart emerged with considerable credit. He spoke rather slowly and precisely and expressed himself clearly and well. Monsieur Spaak admitted to me afterwards that he had not expected to encounter such an interesting and worthwhile *interlocuteur*. As a guest no one could have been easier or more amenable. Michael Stewart subsequently accompanied the Queen on her State Visit to Belgium, and, though I am sure he did not relish the prospect of a good deal of pomp and ceremony, he told me afterwards that he had had a much more interesting time than he had anticipated, and I think he really quite enjoyed it.

When George Brown came to stay with us in Brussels for the first of a series of visits he was preceded by reports of dramas in

* London, 1971.

various other Embassies where he had stayed. It was quite true that life was never dull when he was in the house, and one had to be prepared for the unexpected to happen, but I like to think that his visits to Brussels passed off pretty well. A good deal of the credit for this goes to Jean, who made him feel welcome and at home. On one occasion George and Harold Wilson came together, and that in itself provided an element of tension. It was clear that the Prime Minister must have priority but I had to walk warily! Another visit coincided with one of the crises about the sale of British arms to South Africa, and George felt, with some justice it seemed to me, that decisions of which he disapproved were being deliberately rushed through in his absence. After a series of telephone calls to Denis Healey, who was then on the same side as George Brown (though he appeared to change his position later) and some heated exchanges with 10 Downing Street, a special plane was despatched from London to take George back for an emergency Cabinet meeting. As bad luck would have it, however, Brussels was enveloped in fog and the plane, though distinctly audible overhead, was unable to land. The whole party, including Mrs Brown, had set off for the airport, and Jean and the household staff, for whom such visitations invariably meant a period of long and erratic hours and unexpected demands, had breathed a faint sigh of relief. Then back they all came. This meant of course that all plans for that evening had to be revised and dinner provided for the party before they caught the train for the night ferry.

George had been talking quite openly about the possibility of resignation on this issue of arms for South Africa. At one stage he said rather menacingly to poor Mrs Brown, 'Well, Christmas is off.' This cryptic remark meant that the family party which she was hoping to have at Dorney Wood would not be able to take place because he would have resigned by then and so would no longer be entitled to use the house!

George quite reasonably expected a high standard of food and drink when staying at an Embassy, but he could be generous in his appreciation when everything went as it should. I recall one particular luncheon party at the Brussels Embassy, for Willy Brandt and other NATO Ministers, when our chef had excelled himself, the wine was very good, and the service was as smooth and unobtrusive as it is possible to be. It proved to be a particularly successful occasion from the point of view of making progress on the problems of the moment, and George felt—and said so—that the relaxed and convivial atmosphere, to which he had certainly contributed, had helped to carry things forward.

George Brown had a considerable gift for exposition, and when in form could command the rapt attention of an international gathering. When he and Harold Wilson stayed with us I took them to call on the King of the Belgians, and King Baudouin was much struck by George's explanation of the problems confronting the United Kingdom in Europe. I believe that General de Gaulle was similarly impressed by him, though of course this did not change the General's attitude.

There were, admittedly, some other less happy incidents during George Brown's visits, but following my precept of '*de vivis . . .*' I draw a veil over them.

Whatever Government is in office a visit from one of Her Majesty's Ministers is liable to be a testing experience for an Ambassador, though I took a much more detached view of any eccentricities of behaviour if this Minister came from some Department other than the Foreign Office. There was one such who was so delighted by the custom of kissing the ladies' hands that he carried the practice rather far—up the arm in fact—to the great indignation of the Belgian ladies concerned. There were others who thought they knew so much that they had no need of local advice or guidance. The worst case of this I encountered was a certain lady Minister who had been invited to address the Brussels British Chamber of Commerce Banquet—the first woman ever to have done so. I was not allowed to see her draft speech, and this proved to be a Party-Political address, which was quite unsuited to the occasion, particularly as half those present were Belgians. The longer she went on the more bored her audience became, till at the distant tables there was a good deal of subdued conversation and shuffling of feet. She in turn became increasingly contentious and the speech was really a disaster. The Minister was very cross indeed, supposing that she had been the victim of the ill-manners of a lot of anti-Socialist British businessmen, whereas the root of the trouble was that she had bored to tears a lot of basically well-disposed foreigners by inflicting on them a speech which was of scant interest to them. Another visitor who thought he needed no local guidance or advice was, predictably, Wedgwood Benn. One who then scored high marks, on the other hand, was Denis Healey.

Of the Foreign Ministers of other countries with whom I came in contact, Dean Acheson was certainly one of the most outstanding. I was admittedly prejudiced in his favour because he and his wife were so exceptionally kind to Ernie and Flo Bevin. As a result I saw a good deal of him, not only in official meetings to which I accompanied Ernie, but also on more private occasions in Washington, New York and elsewhere.

As I have already indicated, Dean Acheson had early recognised the value of Ernie as an ally, not only because he represented what was then the most stable and influential power in Western Europe, but because he could also very often bring other European Governments round to his view. Moreover, Dean knew that he was absolutely reliable.

There was much coming and going between the British and American delegations at all international gatherings in those days and the frequent exchanges between the two Secretaries of State were supplemented by constant contact between my American opposite number and myself. From time to time, too, Dean used to pass little notes across to us, commenting on the behaviour of other Foreign Ministers, more often than not the Russians. One which I retained reads as follows: 'Castleregh wrote to his Government from Congress of Vienna re Czar Nicholas: "Acquiescence will not keep him back nor will opposition accelerate his march".'

Dean was on the whole an admirer of the British Foreign Office and on one occasion asked me to go and explain to him exactly how our Private Office operated, since it seemed to him that Ernie always arrived at meetings better briefed than he was. It was quite true that Dean often appeared not to have seen some vital document and had to receive long whispered guidance from members of his delegation. This sometimes obliged him to retract or correct some statement he had just made. On one such occasion he observed, half in irritation and half in amusement, 'Never has an American Secretary of State arrived at an international meeting so badly briefed about so many different subjects.' I did my best to explain how we operated, but the State Department machine was then, and doubtless still is, extremely cumbersome, and I do not think there was ever any possibility of their adopting our system.

Dean Acheson had the skilled lawyer's gift for exposition (he is, perhaps the exception to the rule that good lawyers make bad Foreign Ministers) and it was a pleasure to hear him state a problem or propound possible solutions. He had a very large vocabulary, and, as befitted his ecclesiastical background, a thorough knowledge of both the Bible and the Book of Common Prayer, from which he often quoted. On one occasion, after a particularly regrettable Press leak from the American Delegation he confessed: 'We do earnestly repent, and are heartily sorry for these our misdoings; the remembrance of them is grievous unto us; the burden of them is intolerable.' This at once had the desired effect and Ernie, who had been very cross, was amused and mollified. In Dean's speech at the signing of the North Atlantic Treaty I recognised a quotation from the 46th Psalm, 'Our refuge and strength; a very present help in trouble.'

Dean was sometimes impatient and irritable, and often sarcastic, and he certainly did not suffer fools gladly. This emerged fairly frequently in his dealings with Congress, and I think he often found his own countrymen more troublesome to deal with than foreigners, and in particular the British. He was much more at home with European politicians than any of his immediate predecessors, and his close understanding with Robert Schuman was a considerable asset at a time when the future of Germany was one of the basic problems confronting the Western Powers. The Acheson–Bevin–Schuman collaboration was indeed of the greatest value to the whole Western World in 1949 and 1950, and it is regrettable that nothing like it has existed since.

When in due course Dean was succeeded by another lawyer, Foster Dulles, not only was there a sad falling off in style but we were faced with a stubborn, devious and, as it seemed to me, deplorably narrow-minded politician, with whom no British Minister ever succeeded in establishing a completely happy relationship.

The first Foreign Minister with whom I had to deal as Ambassador was H. C. Hansen who was both Prime Minister and Minister for Foreign Affairs when I arrived in Copenhagen in 1956. One of the first objectives of a newly appointed Ambassador must always be to establish a relationship of mutual confidence with the Minister who will be his most important point of contact with the local Government, and, assuming that relations between the two countries are friendly, he must hope soon to be on close and easy terms with him. Hansen had started life as a manual worker and risen through the Trade Union Movement to be the undisputed leader of the Danish Socialist Party. I soon found that my connection with Ernie Bevin was a useful point in my favour, and I quickly realised that I was lucky in having to deal with such a warm and sympathetic character as H. C. Hansen. On one of our first weekends in Denmark we were invited by the then Danish Ambassador in London to stay in his delightful country house on the Island of Langeland, and he had thoughtfully invited the Hansens to meet us. On the night of our arrival there was an enormous supper party, to which had been bidden the owners of all the great estates round about. All of them were undoubtedly political opponents of H. C. Hansen, but he was an excellent mixer and appeared completely at home in this company. Like nearly all Danes he loved a party and enjoyed good food and drink.

By Sunday evening, helped somewhat by our host's dashing driving, which caused his Jaguar to seize up with a damaged oil-sump, so marooning the three of us on a remote part of the Island, I felt that I knew the Prime Minister pretty well.

Not long after my arrival I had one or two awkward interviews with Hansen on the subject of Suez and despite my best endeavours he clearly found the policies of the British Government incomprehensible. Thereafter, however, we had little cause for disagreement and I soon found that in spite of his comparative inexperience of international affairs his judgment was remarkably sound.

The following year, when the Queen paid her State Visit to Denmark, Hansen took part with enthusiasm in all the functions, and if, as I suspect, he was at heart anti-Monarchist he certainly did not show it. Sad to say, it was not long before he was struck down by cancer. After he had recovered from one major operation I went to see him and he began reminiscing about his early days. He concluded, saying with a smile, 'I have had a wonderfully interesting life so far, and I hope to have a long one'; knowing quite well that this was not to be.

H. C. Hansen's funeral ceremony in Copenhagen Town Hall

was a remarkable occasion, for he had been much liked and admired, but the feature which remains in my memory was the orchestra playing 'Auld Lang Syne' over and over again as the coffin was carried out.

His successor, Jens Otto Krag, was of a very different type. He too was a Socialist, but of a more academic and intellectual variety. Most of my dealings with him were on economic—or fisheries—questions on which he was a considerable expert, and he had a very good understanding of the problems of European economic integration. He had a difficult task during the long period when the attitude of Denmark towards the EEC differed considerably from that of her Scandinavian neighbours. The latter tended to be pretty sharp in their criticisms of the Danish Government and of Krag in particular. Partly, no doubt, because Danish policy was closer to that of the United Kingdom, Krag often seemed to be on better terms with British Ministers and officials than with the Swedes and Norwegians. He was a skilful politician and became a highly competent and experienced Foreign Minister (and later Prime Minister) but for a Dane he was rather reserved and unforthcoming, and though we remained good friends I never succeeded in establishing quite such close relations with him as I had had with H. C. Hansen.

The Foreign Minister whom I perhaps got to know best, and for whose talents I had great admiration, was Paul-Henri Spaak. He first became Belgian Minister for Foreign Affairs when I was serving as Third Secretary at the Embassy in Brussels in 1936. He was then still in his early thirties and had till recently been considered by many of his compatriots to be a dangerous revolutionary. He had already distinguished himself as a fiery political orator and as a leader of demonstrations in the streets of Brussels—a rôle he was to resume in the anti-Leopold riots of the post-liberation period.

In June 1940 we were to meet again at Bordeaux in unusual circumstances. Our Embassy to Belgium had by then disintegrated, the Ambassador, Lancelot Oliphant, and the First Secretary, Peter Scarlett, having both been captured by the Germans in Northern France. Accordingly, when London wished to communicate with the Belgian Government, who after their clash with King Leopold had retreated across France and finally reached Bordeaux, the message had to pass via our Embassy to France. When we had

been for a couple of days in Bordeaux we received a telegram in-
structing us to convey a pressing appeal to the Belgian Government to come to London. In the state of confusion and chaos then
prevailing nobody seemed to know exactly what had become of the
Belgian Government, and it was not until I spotted a Belgian
officer in the street and questioned him as to their whereabouts
that we learnt that they were installed on one of the Congo passenger ships which was in a dock a little way downstream. I was
deputed by the Ambassador to convey the message, and was received by Monsieur Spaak and Monsieur Pierlot, the Prime
Minister, sitting on the deck. They were unable to give me a defi-
nite answer, saying that they must consult their colleagues, and as
I left the ship a steward was walking round ringing a bell which
was doubtless normally a summons to lunch but was now intended
to call together the Cabinet.

In the event, the Belgians, learning that the French Government
were proposing to move to North Africa—a plan which they soon
abandoned—set off themselves for the Mediterranean coast, but
never got there. After various extraordinary adventures Monsieur
Spaak and several of his colleagues eventually reached London via
Spain and Portugal, and he became a key figure in the Government in exile.

I saw quite a lot of Monsieur Spaak during my time as Private
Secretary to Ernie Bevin, and then again during our negotiations
with the EEC in 1961–3. The chief Belgian ministerial spokesman
during the Brussels negotiations was Monsieur Fayat, but Monsieur Spaak put in an appearance from time to time, and on the
night of the final breakdown he was present to make an eloquent
and effective attack on the behaviour of de Gaulle and his Government.

When I returned to Brussels as Ambassador in 1963, Monsieur
Spaak was still Foreign Minister, a rôle he had filled with only a
few gaps for the last twenty-seven years. He had of course meanwhile become a distinguished international statesman, being famous
not least as one of the founders of the European Economic Community. Indeed, without his drive and imagination the negotiations for the Treaty of Rome might never have succeeded.

It was always a pleasant duty to have to go to see Paul-Henri
Spaak to discuss some common problem. In the period following

my arrival to Brussels he was often disappointed by the rather negative attitude of the British Government on European questions, but at least we were not being as obstructive as General de Gaulle. In any case, our discussions were always extremely friendly, and an exchange of views with him was always stimulating.

Monsieur Spaak was an eloquent public speaker and dwarfed everyone else in the Belgian Parliament, and indeed in the country as a whole. After the death of Winston Churchill he paid a splendid tribute to him before a large and sympathetic audience, while on less serious occasions he could be extremely witty and amusing. He did not care for large and formal parties—though he greatly enjoyed good food and drink, which he consumed at remarkable speed, and a game of bridge. If one could get him to a small gathering he would entertain the whole company with a fund of stories and anecdotes from his colourful career, and no meal at which he was present was ever dull.

Monsieur Spaak was an outspoken critic of Gaullist policies, and the General did not appreciate this. One French Ambassador in Brussels was removed from his post and never re-employed because he was considered to have been on too friendly terms with Monsieur Spaak. His successor was determined not to suffer the same fate, and Monsieur Spaak once confided to me that he had not seen the man officially for a year on end—an extraordinary state of affairs considering the great number of interests which France and Belgium had in common.

It was rather surprising, in view of his generally critical attitude towards French policies, that, as related in another chapter, Monsieur Spaak did not approve of our plans for the commemoration of the 150th Anniversary of the Battle of Waterloo, which he apparently thought were provocative to the French. This view was certainly not shared by the great majority of his compatriots, but he elected to stay away from our Waterloo Ball and from other ceremonies at that time.

Apart from European questions the subject which took up most time during Monsieur Spaak's latter years as Foreign Minister was the Congo, which, after attaining independence in 1960, passed through a very turbulent phase. By his convincing defence of Belgian policy at the United Nations Monsieur Spaak did much to improve his country's somewhat tarnished reputation there. At the time of the Stanleyville Rebellion in 1966 he showed great courage in accepting responsibility for sending Belgian paratroops into the Congo to restore order. Fortunately the operation was a conspicuous success and saved many lives, but if it had gone wrong he would have been much criticised.

In spite of the years he spent in London during the war, Monsieur Spaak never mastered the English language, and though he could understand a fair amount he really could not speak it at all. He was also quite unable to speak Flemish, which, for one who had been Prime Minister of Belgium, was surprising.

Monsieur Spaak, who had been a doughty fighter in his youth, mellowed greatly in his later years, and it was difficult to recognise in him the zealous young Socialist of the pre-war period. He became fairly disillusioned about Belgian party politics and frustrated by the interminable linguistic disputes. He finally ceased to be an active member of the Belgian Socialist Party and later accepted an appointment as a consultant with an American international corporation, but devoted much of his time to writing his memoirs.

It was generally agreed in Belgium that when Monsieur Spaak finally retired he would be a very difficult man to follow. In the event Monsieur Pierre Harmel, who took his place and continued as Belgian Foreign Minister for the next eight years, though a man of totally different stamp, proved a very worthy successor. He had been a Professor at Liège University and was a devout Catholic. He was highly intelligent and a very pleasant person with whom to do business. In Whitehall he was sometimes accused of being devious and Jesuitical, and in his desire to find compromise solutions for the problems dividing the principal members of the Common Market or of NATO he was possibly inclined to carry his efforts at mediation too far. But he was basically a very sincere man and I always found him reliable. He consistently strove to bring about a détente between East and West, and had quite an influence on the evolution of NATO thought in this direction. All in all he ensured that Belgium's voice in the various international organisations was listened to with respect.

7

AMBASSADORIAL CHIEFS; THE FALL OF FRANCE, JUNE 1940

AN UNUSUAL FEATURE of my diplomatic career was that I only served under four Ambassadors, and one of these, Lord Halifax, was clearly a rather special case so that it seemed more appropriate to include him with other Foreign Secretaries in the previous chapter.

When I went to the Embassy in Brussels as Third Secretary in 1932 a new Ambassador was about to arrive in the person of Sir George Clerk. The Counsellor, Nevile Bland,* and I, arrayed in top hats and morning coats went to the station to meet him and when he emerged from the train he looked the complete stage Ambassador—tall and distinguished with silvery hair and a monocle. He was very much one of the old school. He had previously been for many years Ambassador to Turkey where he had succeeded in establishing close personal relations with Ataturk, with whom he used to play poker into the early hours of the morning. I think that he regarded Brussels as rather a come-down, and anyhow, before he had been there many weeks he was told that he was going to be moved to Paris, so that he ceased to take any great interest in his mission to Belgium. His wife was an imposing lady, both in appearance and manner, and during her short stay she managed to make herself fairly unpopular with the senior members of the Embassy staff. She was anyhow more interested in her painting and in spiritualism than in running an Embassy. Though I personally had no cause for complaint and indeed I had learnt one or two useful lessons from this slightly intimidating couple, there were no great regrets when the Clerks moved on to Paris.

My next Chief was Sir Esmond Ovey, who had previously been Ambassador in Moscow and had been recalled at the time of the

* Later Sir Nevile Bland, H.M. Ambassador to the Netherlands.

Metro-Vickers Trial a year or so before. He was a much more easy-going and approachable character, and whereas the Clerks had only just been on speaking terms with each other he was devoted to his charming part-French, part-Latin American second wife. Esmond Ovey did not take his duties too seriously and was never one to look for work, so that he managed to spend a great deal of time on the golf course. We had one very hard winter when our Chancery hours were adjusted to enable the Oveys and any members of the staff who could skate to play amateurish but spirited ice-hockey on a frozen lake in the Forêt de Soignes, just outside Brussels. If the weather was very inclement he resorted to billiards or other indoor games. One favourite sport consisted in organising dog steeplechases down the corridors of the Embassy. I have to admit that at the Copenhagen Embassy we had some rather similar forms of entertainment, one of which was a dog's treasure hunt—for a hidden lump of sugar. This was a very popular game with our two dachshunds. Another was a form of follow-my-leader with the dachshunds in full cry on a circular course through various rooms including the ballroom. This always caused much hilarity and we were urged by visiting members of the Royal Household to organise a performance for the benefit of the Queen when she came to see the Embassy. We were tempted to do so but decided that it was not quite the right occasion.

Esmond Ovey was an excellent host and very good company, and as a couple the Oveys were much liked by their junior staff, including ourselves. We boldly invited them to dinner one evening, but this was rather a disaster as our normally competent cook seemed to be overcome by the occasion and something went wrong with every course, from the soup which was too salty to the cheese fritters which were heavy as lead.

When, in February 1940, we arrived at the Embassy in Paris, I found myself working under a very different type of chief, Sir Ronald Campbell. There were then two Sir Ronald Campbells in the Diplomatic Service, the other, who had recently been appointed Ambassador in Belgrade and with whom Ernie Bevin and I later stayed in Cairo, being generally known as Little Ronnie. They were in fact both short of stature and at first sight my new Ambassador might not have appeared very imposing. He was, however, very far from being a lightweight, and on the contrary, was not only highly competent professionally but a strong and very determined personality.

First impressions on our side, both of the Ambassador and of Lady Campbell, were very favourable, though I found him slightly intimidating. Our first dinner party at the Embassy began badly. In the course of my official career I was very seldom late on any occasion that mattered, though, being given to over-optimism I often ran things rather fine. On this occasion I had not made sufficient allowance for Paris traffic problems and we arrived a minute or two after the appointed hour to find that the principal guest, who was Lord Gort, the Commander-in-Chief of the British Expeditionary Force, had unfortunately got there first. I was conscious of a slight cloud of disapproval, and took great care never to be late again.

The Chancery was then established in rather cramped quarters in what had once been the Embassy stables and we had to walk across the courtyard in order to reach the Ambassador's study in the Residence. The Chancery staff was surprisingly small, consisting of the Counsellor, Hal Mack,* myself and the two junior secretaries, Donald Maclean (of whom I have written in chapter 5) and Henry Hankey,† who were shortly joined by an Honorary Attaché (a now extinct species) in the person of Anthony Nutting.‡ The Minister was Oliver Harvey,§ who after the war was to return as Ambassador.

During the next couple of months—the last part of the 'phoney war' period—my work was sometimes of considerable interest, notably when it involved the discussion of politico–strategic issues with officials of the Quai d'Orsay. There were also numerous important visitors to the Embassy, including Malcolm McDonald, Herbert Morrison and Harold Nicolson, whom I had to help look after, but an inordinate amount of all the Secretaries' time was taken up by the laborious task of cyphering and decyphering telegrams. At that period there was a rule that telegrams of a secret

* Later Sir H. Mack, Ambassador to the Argentine.
† The Hon. H. A. H. Hankey, now an Assistant Under Secretary of State in the F.C.O.
‡ Now Sir Anthony Nutting, Bart., at one time Minister of State at the Foreign Office.
§ Later Lord Harvey of Tasburgh.

character had to be dealt with by the diplomatic staff, and though we became pretty adept it was a time-consuming occupation and involved us in many late night sessions.

Paris in the early spring of 1940 was in some ways still surprisingly normal. Restaurants and theatres were full and there were no shortages of any kind, but social life was on a much reduced scale and there was little diplomatic entertaining. By the middle of March Jean had returned to the family in Scotland, having first helped to get me installed in our furnished flat in the Avenue St Honoré d'Eylau, with an excellent maid, Alice, to cook and look after me. The Chancery normally worked over weekends, and though I occasionally drove out into the country for a walk on a Sunday afternoon there was no possibility of going further afield.

Anglo-French relations at this time were not altogether easy. The Russo-Finnish war with its awkward political repercussions had been a major preoccupation when I first got to Paris, but in the middle of March hostilities came to an end. There had been little that we or the French could do to help the Finns and this had increased the mood of frustration in France and led to the fall of Daladier's Government and to his replacement by Paul Reynaud. French opposition to British plans for laying mines in the Rhine began to cause increasing irritation in London while the German invasion of Denmark and Norway on 9 April imposed fresh strains on the alliance. The battles of Narvik and the fluctuating fortunes of the Norwegian campaign aroused alternating hope and gloom, and while there was plenty of evidence of German drive and efficiency, stories began to filter through of allied muddle and incompetence. The final evacuation inevitably led to a further outbreak of criticism in France.

Meanwhile everyone had for long been awaiting the day when the Germans launched their offensive on the Western Front, and when it finally came on 10 May it was almost a relief that the period of expectancy was over. We had all been led to believe that the Maginot Line was impregnable—perhaps it was, because it was never put to the test—and the accepted doctrine was that the highly trained French armies, which together with the British Expeditionary Force manned the rest of the line to the Channel coast, were ready to tackle anything that the Germans could send against them. It was true that there were pessimists who had cast doubt on the state of morale and fighting value of the French troops, and the success of the Germans in Norway had been discouraging, but there were very few who foresaw the extent of the disasters which occurred in the fortnight following the German invasion.

Meanwhile, the French internal situation was worrying, and it was common knowledge that there was a strong current of defeatism among leading politicians. The Ambassador had already sent home a very pessimistic report, drawing attention to the danger that those who were prepared to do a deal with the Germans might gain power in the event of a military disaster. But as I have said, there were few people at that time who were expecting this to occur.

On 16 May, after barely a week of fighting, Monsieur Reynaud told the Ambassador that the German tanks had broken through and were advancing so rapidly that he could not be sure that they would not be at the gates of Paris within twenty-four hours. Churchill had come to Paris for a meeting of the Supreme War Council that afternoon and in the light of the information given by the French, he agreed with the Ambassador that all the wives and lady members of the staff should be sent home forthwith. They were packed into cars in the darkened Embassy courtyard at 11.30 that night, and despatched, protesting bitterly, with our two Honorary Attachés as escorts, to Le Havre whence they were shipped back to England. Meanwhile we had begun to burn the most important of our secret archives. We had no modern equipment for this purpose and at the outset we carried bundles of papers across the courtyard to the Embassy stokehole, where, by about 4 a.m. we had disposed of our most sensitive selection. Burning concentrated masses of paper is at best a slow and laborious occupation, and since no one had had the forethought to reduce the volume of our archives we discovered that these covered a period of twenty-five years, including the last Peace Conference. For the next five days we had enormous bonfires in the Embassy garden, whence a gust of wind would occasionally blow a half-charred sheet of paper out onto the Champs-Elysées. I doubt whether any German agent lurking there would have acquired any valuable information.

In the event the German tanks did not of course make directly for Paris but turned instead towards the Channel ports, so that we now had a brief respite. It was a period of almost undiluted gloom, the one slightly cheering episode being the relative success of the Dunkirk evacuation. While this was in progress there was another meeting in Paris of the Supreme War Council, and one of my memories is of a member of the War Cabinet Secretariat telephoning from the Chancery to a colleague in London and chattering away in Hindustani, which constituted a simple and relatively secure cypher since anyone tapping our telephones was most unlikely to understand what was being said. The score of successful evacuations from Dunkirk was passed to us under the cover of being someone's new telephone number.

During this period we received frequent personal messages from Winston, addressed either to Reynaud or Daladier (now Minister of War) containing not only exhortations aimed at encouraging a mood of resistance but also some characteristic personal suggestions about how French villages should be defended and the German tanks frustrated. These we had to translate, and putting Churchillian communications of this kind into idiomatic French was quite a test. Between us in the Chancery we could produce a more or less adequate French version, but the Ambassador's French was unquestionably of a higher standard than ours and he could always improve on our prose.

We sometimes found ourselves having to take urgent communications round to Reynaud's flat in the middle of the night. If so we were liable to be received by his mistress, Madame de Portes, a notorious character who was known to be completely defeatist. We were later to encounter her at Tours and again at Bordeaux and her influence on Reynaud was consistently nefarious.

The Ambassador, being now alone, apart from the servants, in his vast house, took to inviting two or three of us over to join him for lunch every day. We always had an extremely good meal, but conversation was not easy, and when the news was bad, as it nearly always was, the Ambassador tended to relapse into gloomy silence. When we did not go across to the house for lunch we usually had trays brought over to the Chancery from the Embassy kitchens so as to be able to eat at our desks, and this frequently happened in the evenings too, as all too often we were unable to go out owing to the flood of telegrams requiring attention.

Our delightful Military Attaché, Malise Graham,* who went to daily briefings at the Ministry of War, had his own technique for passing on to us what he had heard. 'The situation is not too good,' he would say, 'really not good at all; in fact it's about as bad as it possibly could be.'

Meanwhile, there had been a little desultory bombing of the Paris suburbs, and from the balcony of my flat I had had a grandstand view of the German air attack on the Renault works. It was clear that as soon as the Germans were ready to move on Paris there was little to stop them, and it was only a matter of time before the capital had to be evacuated. The French plan was to move the seat of Government to Tours, and we, like the other Embassies, had been allocated a château in the neighbourhood in case it became necessary to leave Paris. On Sunday, 9 June, we discovered that the French, without telling us, were engaged in evacuating most of the Ministries, and the Ambassador decided to send an advance party from the Embassy, of which I was to be in charge, down to our château at Champchevrier, about fifteen miles northwest of Tours, the following day.

Next morning, having packed up my flat as far as possible and loaded a few of my belongings into my car, I said goodbye to Alice, who would gladly have come with me, and went to collect Tony Nutting who had been earmarked as my companion on the journey. By now the exodus from Paris was in full swing and all the routes to the west were in a chaotic state. At times we made quite good progress but at others we got held up by the streams of refugees travelling in private cars, lorries, farm carts of all descriptions, or just walking or bicycling along with packs on their backs. Many cars had run out of petrol which was now quite unobtainable except for those like ourselves who had special supplies reserved at strategic points. Fortunately the weather was absolutely perfect so that for the many who had to sleep by the roadside no great hardship was involved.

Tony and I reached Tours in the late afternoon, and having called on the Prefet of the Department to inform him of our arrival we went on to our château which neither of us had previously seen. We were received by the owner, an old lady of about seventy who

* General Lord Malise Graham.

was dressed all in black except for white tennis shoes. She was naturally somewhat overwhelmed by the prospect of the Embassy's arrival, but was prepared to make the best of it and soon had her staff running to and fro helping to get the rooms ready.

The château was a splendid sixteenth-century building surrounded by a moat, and Louis XIII had reputedly stayed there when on a hunting expedition. It contained beautiful tapestries and some fine furniture, but the plumbing was primitive in the extreme, and though there were two baths not even the cold water taps would run. It was agreed that the old lady and her family, including several grandchildren, should continue to occupy one wing of the house, but there was still room in it for sixteen members of the Embassy staff—not counting chauffeurs, messengers, etc., who were to be accommodated in the stable block. The village was also at our disposal and some of the Embassy departments were to be billeted there.

There was only one very old-fashioned telephone in the house and, perhaps unwisely, I took as my room the library where it was situated. The local Exchange was chaotic but I was eventually able to telephone through to the Embassy in Paris and learned that the Ambassador and the remaining members of the staff were about to leave and should arrive at Champchevrier in the early hours of the morning.

I now found myself acting rather like a hotel receptionist. Cars drew up at intervals during the night and I had to deal with each in turn, conducting to their rooms those to whom I had allocated beds in the château and directing others to billets in the village. The Ambassador arrived at about four a.m. and the final contingent turned up for breakfast. Only Henry Hankey was missing, one of the cars having had a minor accident and he having volunteered to stay while it was repaired.

The next day was spent largely in getting ourselves organised and we were soon equipped to receive and despatch telegrams. The Ambassador went to call at the Ministry of Foreign Affairs, who were established in another château about twenty kilometres away, but found it extremely difficult to discover what was going on. At our château we all worked in the salon, the Ambassador sitting in one corner drafting telegrams while the rest of us decyphered or dealt with other correspondence at tables dotted around the room.

We all had our meals at one large table in the dining room, presided over by the Ambassador.

There were air raids on Tours during the night and one or two planes which we presumed to be German flew low over the château. The next day was relatively calm, though it was clear that the military situation was rapidly deteriorating and we learned that the Germans had reached the Seine. Oliver Harvey and I went to exchange views with the two Commonwealth colleagues, the Canadians and South Africans, who were established in lesser châteaux not far away.

Thursday, 13 June, was a day of drama. Winston Churchill had paid a flying visit to the French High Command at Briare on the night of 11–12 June, and we now learned that he was flying out again for a meeting of the Supreme War Council at Tours. We did not receive sufficient notice to be able to meet him and his party and neither was any French official representative at the bomb-damaged airport to greet him. We had however seen the escorting squadron of Hurricanes from Champchevrier and the Ambassador managed to get to the Prefecture in Tours at about the same time as the French Ministers who were summoned to the meeting. It was on this occasion that Monsieur Reynaud first put forward the request that France should be released from her undertaking not to conclude a separate peace—a request which Churchill was not prepared to concede. I drove into Tours during the afternoon with new telegrams for the Ambassador, and it then appeared that the Prime Minister and his staff might come to spend the night at our château. This was a stirring prospect but it would have been none too easy to accommodate and feed such a party. In any case the Prime Minister later decided that he must get back to London.

That evening the French Government decided that they must leave Tours for Bordeaux and at about midnight General Spears, who was now attached to Monsieur Reynaud, arrived at Champchevrier with a message to the effect that the German tanks were advancing so rapidly that we had better cross to the south side of the Loire by 10 o'clock the next morning or we might not get across at all. I went round the château warning people to be prepared for an early start and we then set to work to pack up a few essential papers and equipment while other papers were destroyed. After about three hours' sleep I was woken up at a very early hour by a knocking on my window, and found it was the South African Minister who had come round to seek advice on his future movements. The answer was of course that he, like ourselves, should now make for Bordeaux.

The following morning we packed up our personal belongings and wrote our names in the Baronne's visitors' book. I think in the end she was sorry to see us go, the more so since it seemed all too likely that we would soon be replaced by Germans. We eventually set off in a convoy of ten cars headed by the Ambassador's Rolls and including also a Rolls belonging to Lord Derby, which had been in Paris and had been put at the Embassy's disposal.

We had been concerned about the fate of Henry Hankey who had failed to show up at Champchevrier or to communicate with us, and we rather feared that he must have been overtaken on the road by the Germans. However, as we were approaching the bridge over the Loire a small figure on a blue and yellow bicycle was seen coming towards us, and this proved to be Henry. He was most reluctant to abandon his bicycle, which he said had saved his life and might well come in useful again, but no one was prepared to have it tied on to their well-laden car, and it was left by the roadside.

After leaving Tours we soon got heavily involved in refugee traffic and my car and Lord Derby's Rolls got separated from the rest. The likelihood of reaching Bordeaux that night seemed remote, but we turned off down side roads and soon began to make better progress. We had taken the precaution of supplying ourselves with some Air Force rations before leaving, and though food was almost unobtainable we found a village shop where we succeeded in buying some bread and fruit. We also had with us some remaining bottles of champagne and in the end had rather a good picnic sitting in the shade by the roadside.

We finally reached Bordeaux about 9 o'clock that night. We made for the British Consulate where we learnt that most of the Embassy staff were being billeted at the inconveniently remote Château Filhot (famous for its Sauternes), but that a few rooms had been commandeered for the Ambassador and key members of the party at the Hotel Montré in the middle of Bordeaux. I annexed one of these rooms and had my only really good night's sleep between leaving Paris and our final departure from France.

Next morning, after breakfast and a bath—my first since leaving Paris—I went round to the Consulate where there was a scene of utter confusion. There were long queues of people seeking help or advice, the majority of them being British subjects who wanted to be told what to do in order to be evacuated to the United Kingdom. There were others who could not make up their minds whether they wanted to leave or to stay. There were also large numbers of foreigners of various nationalities, but in particular Poles, Czechs and refugee-Germans and Austrians, all of whom were clamouring for visas or permits for Britain. They varied from Ministers and senior officials to others with no credentials of any kind, and it was not easy to decide who were genuine and deserving of help and who were potential fifth-columnists.

The British subjects were primarily the responsibility of the British Consulate, though the Consul and his small staff were ill-equipped to deal with a crisis of this magnitude and we inevitably became involved, at least when problems of policy arose. The Chancery were responsible for dealing with the foreigners and with individual Frenchmen who turned to us for help in getting out of the country. Among others with whom I personally became involved were King Zog of Albania and his family. His tough-looking Chamberlain had charge of some extremely heavy boxes which presumably contained bars of gold or the Crown Jewels. He was not alone, during those hectic days, in giving the impression that anyone who proved helpful over permits, etc. could expect a suitable reward! For quite a few, particularly among the German Jewish refugees, whether they got out of the country or not might be literally a matter of life and death. One could not therefore blame them for the emotional way in which they pressed their claims.

During the next few days I went round once or twice to see members of the Ministry for Foreign Affairs who were established in wretched conditions in a school. They, however, were now powerless and the only way to have any useful discussion with the French Authorities was for the Ambassador to go and see members of the Government. Meanwhile, one of the chief occupations of the diminished Chancery staff throughout the next week remained the encyphering or decyphering of telegrams. These were often of the utmost urgency and many dealt with matters of great moment

K

such as the future of the French fleet. The telegraph was by now our only means of communication with London, and since there was some doubt about which routes had been cut or were being jammed we took to sending our messages by cable via New York with a duplicate despatched, so long as there was a British warship in Bordeaux, by wireless to the Admiralty.

On the day we left Paris Donald Maclean had—very tiresomely as we thought—got married to Melinda Marling, an American girl with whom he had been having a brief affair. We had told them that they had better fend for themselves and arrange to get back to the United Kingdom as best they could. After various adventures they turned up at Bordeaux, and, since they had nowhere to sleep and accommodation was unobtainable, I generously gave up my room to them (little suspecting that he was an actual or potential spy). I never got my room back, and from then on shared another room, which contained a divan as well as two beds, with Henry and Tony. This room soon became the sole office of the Embassy, where telegrams were dealt with and telephone messages received, and here the few remaining members of the staff tended to foregather to exchange news. In the mornings when the beds were still unmade and the remains of breakfast lay on the table it was not exactly a spic and span Chancery.

Meanwhile all those members of the staff who had been billeted at the Château Filhot and who were not regarded as essential were, together with the Macleans, embarked on one of the ships which were evacuating British subjects to the United Kingdom. The Consulate had been closed and from now on our party was reduced to the Ambassador, the Minister, Hal Mack, Henry, Tony and myself, together with the Service Attachés and the Canadian and South African Ministers, who no longer had any staff and very naturally attached themselves to us.

It was impossible to get food (other than breakfast) in our hotel, and most restaurants were running short, but just opposite was the 'Chapon Fin', then one of the most famous restaurants in France, which seemed able to conjure up supplies from somewhere, and this from now on became our regular eating place. It was also the normal rendezvous of members of the American Embassy and of officials from the Ministry for Foreign Affairs as well as of an assortment of French politicians varying from Monsieur Mandel, one of the chief of those who favoured continued resistance, to Monsieur Laval, the arch-defeatist.

The French political situation was becoming increasingly depressing. On 16 June London produced the hastily devised plan for a form of Anglo-French union. This seemed to us a fairly wild idea but in any case it was clear that the situation in France had deteriorated to an extent which made the serious examination of such a far-reaching project quite impossible. The immediate effect on Reynaud was favourable, but it was much too late for it to affect the course of events, and that afternoon, following a gloomy meeting of his Cabinet, Reynaud resigned. He was replaced by a Government headed by Marshal Pétain, which excluded all those Ministers who had favoured continued resistance. Very late that night I went round with the Ambassador to the President's temporary quarters where the new Cabinet had just been meeting. The Ambassador then had a very rough interview with the new Minister for Foreign Affairs, Monsieur Baudouin, who informed him that the Government had decided to ask the Germans for terms for an armistice. The Ambassador insisted then, and confirmed this later in writing, that we expected to be consulted as soon as any reply was received.

From now on our attention was concentrated on two main issues, which were to some extent interconnected. First, what was to happen to the powerful French fleet, and second, was there still an outside chance of a French Government of sorts being established in North Africa and carrying on the war from there? The discussions about the French fleet tended to become increasingly confused. On 18 June the First Lord of the Admiralty, A. V. Alexander, accompanied by the First Sea Lord, arrived in Bordeaux charged to try to obtain assurances that in no circumstances would the French ships be allowed to fall into German hands. They were given what appeared to be satisfactory undertakings by Marshal Pétain and Admiral Darlan (confirming those already given to the Ambassador), but we had no confidence that the French would be able to resist German pressure. The next day Lord Lloyd arrived from London with messages from the Prime Minister aimed at improving the morale of the new French Government. There seemed, indeed, at this stage to be a slight lightening of the atmosphere, and on 20 June we were informed that the French Government had decided to move to Perpignan en route for North

Africa, where they hoped to establish themselves. At this point the Ambassador decided that he, together with a few members of the staff, should accompany the French Government, while the rest of the party were to be sent back to the United Kingdom on a British warship. We packed up once again, and the Ambassador's party was actually due to leave in half an hour when we received a message saying that the Government had decided after all to stay in Bordeaux. It was clear that this was a bad sign and it meant in fact that all idea of further resistance to the Germans had been abandoned.

Those French politicians who had continued to oppose a policy of surrender now found themselves in an increasingly difficult situation. A number of them had embarked in a ship which had been destined to take them to North Africa but had got no further than Le Verdon. Those who remained in Bordeaux were in some danger from their own new Government which at one stage had caused Monsieur Mandel to be arrested. One evening I received a telephone message asking me to go to see Monsieur Herriot at his private house where I found him closeted with Monsieur Blum. They wanted the Embassy to help evacuate some of their friends who were particularly compromised. I replied that we would do our best, but what about the two of them? Monsieur Blum in particular, being a Jew, was obviously liable to be arrested when the Germans arrived, if not before. He paced up and down the room, torn by conflicting feelings, but like Monsieur Herriot came to the conclusion that it was his duty to stay in France, and though grateful for my offer to help arrange for their departure to London they both declined.

Meanwhile, there had been several air-raids on Bordeaux. Compared to the raids on London in the following winter these were very minor affairs, but they made quite an impression at the time, and one bomb fell near enough to our hotel to cause all the lights to go out. The Ambassador continued drafting telegrams by the light of a candle, while the rest of us went on with our apparently never-ending task of decyphering at another table, also by candlelight.

Soon after midnight on the night of 21–2 June I received a telephone call from the Minister for Foreign Affairs saying that the German Armistice terms had been received, and adding that after they had been considered by the Cabinet at 1 a.m. he would be ready to see Sir Ronald Campbell. As soon as the latter heard this he decided that he must get hold of the terms as soon as possible, and set off for the President's house, where, after an angry scene he succeeded in extracting a copy of the document from the reluctant Baudouin. From then until 10 o'clock the following morning we were engaged without respite in encyphering a series of 'most immediate' telegrams containing the actual armistice terms together with the Ambassador's comments and explanations.

We had little doubt that the French Government would accept and sign, and this meant that the Germans would soon be in complete control. There were rumours that the spearheads of the advancing German armies were now close, and people were quite prepared to see German tanks crossing the bridge into Bordeaux at any moment. Meanwhile, French soldiers were selling their equipment in the market place. It seemed clear that the Embassy's mission was nearly over and that there was little more that we could do. We had a final lunch at the Chapon Fin, where the patron produced some of his rarest wines for our benefit, and then prepared to leave that evening. As we were engaged in packing up, the Ambassador walked into our office saying, 'I have one further telegram to send', and wrote down the two words, 'Armistice signed'.

The Ambassador went round to pay farewell calls on Pétain and Baudouin, and we did not finally leave until nearly midnight. As usual, I had Tony Nutting as my passenger, but he immediately went to sleep and I had great difficulty in not doing so too, for not only had we had no sleep the night before but for the past week we had usually been up till 2 or 3 o'clock in the morning, while twice I noted that it was after 5 o'clock before I got to bed. Though I remember hitting the grass verge once or twice we somehow managed to reach our destination which was a palatial villa near the shore at Arcachon.

It had always been contemplated that if and when the time came for us to be evacuated a cruiser would be made available to take us back to England, but enemy mining had now made the Gironde unsafe and the last British destroyer, HMS *Berkeley*, had left Bordeaux two or three days previously. The plan now was that we should be picked up by the Navy off Arcachon the following morning. The officer who was in charge of the shore end of this operation was Ian Fleming, and there was something faintly James Bond-like about the marble-halled villa, and indeed the whole evacuation plan.

Early next morning, after a few hours sleep, we drove down to the beach, where we abandoned all our cars, and, escorted by a young British naval officer and two ratings, embarked in one of the local sardine fishing boats which had been commandeered for the occasion. We learned afterwards that one of the French chauffeurs who stayed behind decided that the Ambassador's beautiful new Rolls, which incidentally had the Royal coat-of-arms on the door, could not just be left on the shore. Not knowing quite what to do, he decided to drive it back to Paris, and, passing through the advancing German armies, finally left it in the Embassy courtyard where it was safe under the protection of the Americans.

After the experiences of the past weeks, which had been in many ways thankless and disillusioning, we were all glad enough to be leaving French soil. For the last few days at any rate we had known that the German advance guards could not be very far away, and we had no wish to be put in the bag (like Sir Lancelot Oliphant, the British Ambassador to Belgium). We were a bedraggled looking party, dead tired, hungry—for most of us had had no breakfast —and to make matters worse it was pouring with rain. We had no protection on our fishing boat other than a large tarpaulin, under which we sat huddled beside our suitcases. Moreover, once we got outside the harbour we found that it was decidedly rough, and, though I am fortunately a good sailor, this could certainly not be said of some of the other members of the party, notably of the Canadian Minister, General Vanier (the future Governor General). The strong aroma of sardines made matters worse.

We had hoped that we would quite quickly be picked up by the cruiser, HMS *Galatea*, which had been deputed to take us back to England, and it was discouraging to find no sign of her. It was known that there were enemy submarines lurking in those waters so we began to fear that she might have been sunk. Our fishing boat was not equipped for a long journey in rough seas but on the other hand the prospect of being obliged to go ashore again was not at all attractive. It was not until we had been tossing about for more than three hours that we were finally able to pick up a wireless message saying that a destroyer was on its way to collect us.

In spite of our general state of exhaustion and despondency I think we all of us felt great sympathy for the Ambassador. It was a tragic end to his mission to France, which had begun with such high hopes and expectations less than a year before. He was probably wondering, too, whether he should perhaps after all have stayed on in Bordeaux, and questioning whether there was anything more that he could conceivably have done to stiffen French resistance to the German terms, or at least to ensure some more satisfactory arrangement with regard to the French fleet.

However, all that was now quite beyond our control, and the appearance through the driving rain of HMS *Fraser*, a Canadian destroyer, brought about an immediate improvement in morale. We were soon all taken aboard, though not without some difficulty in view of the heavy swell, particularly when it came to the turn of poor Vanier, who, in addition to being extremely seasick, had a wooden leg and in the end had to be hauled on board like a sack of coal.

We, or at any rate most of us, felt very much better when we had had something hot to eat and drink and in no time I was fast asleep. We now proceeded at speed down to St Jean de Luz where HMS *Galatea* was awaiting us, and later that afternoon we were all duly transhipped on to the cruiser. Sad to say the *Fraser*, on which we had been so hospitably received, was sunk in a collision a night or two later with heavy loss of life.

The harbour at St Jean de Luz was full of shipping, most of which had been diverted there in order to pick up refugees or Polish troops who were waiting to be evacuated to the United Kingdom. The Poles, many of whom had been involved in the fighting in eastern France and were in a state of exhaustion, were encamped with their weapons on the quayside, patiently awaiting their turn to be ferried out to the ships which were anchored a little way out in the harbour. When I went ashore, as I did soon after our arrival, I could not help being struck by the attitude of these men who had come so far from their homes but whose one wish seemed to be to be able to resume the fight against the Germans as soon as possible.

The Ambassador had meanwhile received a final telegram requesting him to convey a message from the King to the French President, offering sympathy but urging him to do what he could to help us over the French fleet. It was not quite clear how these instructions were to be carried out, and I was deputed to go ashore and do the best I could. The message contained nothing of a secret nature so that the solution seemed to be to forward it as part of a personal message from the Ambassador to the President, but it was Sunday evening, and accordingly all Post Offices were closed. I decided to call on the Mayor and enlist his help, and he in fact proved most obliging and was able to make special arrangements for the despatch of my telegram which he readily agreed was a somewhat exceptional one. I had dinner at a restaurant beside the harbour with the naval officer who had accompanied me, and we were finally collected and taken back to the ship shortly before she was due to sail.

Most of the journey back from St Jean de Luz to Plymouth was spent in either sleeping or eating. The next morning a telegram was received from Lord Halifax, addressed to the Ambassador, which read: 'Please accept the grateful thanks of my colleagues and myself for your unremitting labours in the Allied Cause, performed towards the end in conditions of danger, discomfort and acute personal embarrassment. Your work and that of your staff has been beyond praise.' This message gave all of us great satisfaction, and it must have been particularly comforting to the Ambassador to be reassured that his really superhuman efforts to save something from the wreck had been duly recognised at home.

We had no further adventures on our way back, though it continued to be pretty rough. When we reached Plymouth we were all put into first-class sleepers on the night train to London. We were given a very warm welcome at the Foreign Office, and after two days spent in drafting a despatch recording our doings during the final stages in Bordeaux I was told I could have ten days' leave, and set off to join the family in Scotland.

After having been Ambassador in Paris there was not likely to be any other job for Sir Ronald Campbell which would not seem something of a come-down. For the next few months he was employed in Whitehall on various minor jobs relating to Anglo-French relations and was then appointed Ambassador to Lisbon. Now that the Germans had overrun such a large part of the Continent of Europe, Lisbon, like Madrid, had assumed unusual importance, and I think he was glad to have another Embassy. All the same, Lisbon is not Paris, and poor Ronnie Campbell must frequently have reflected that he had been very unlucky in that, having attained the one post which he had coveted above all others, the fortunes of war had dictated that his time there should be so short and that he should be obliged to leave the country in such tragic and depressing circumstances.

8

ROYAL AND OTHER OCCASIONS

HAVING SERVED as Ambassador to two of the slowly dwindling number of monarchies, and having been involved, as Private Secretary or in other capacities, in sundry state occasions in this country, I have had more to do both with our own and with foreign royal families than is now normal for a member of the Diplomatic Service. The Queen paid State Visits to both Copenhagen and Brussels during my period as Ambassador, and I was of course deeply involved on each occasion. As far as I could establish, only one British Ambassador before me had been at the receiving end for two State Visits, and that was in the reign of King Edward VII. There has been one other since: John Russell,* who was responsible for helping to organise two colourful visits—those to Addis Ababa and Rio.

My first encounters with Royalty, apart from attending what was then the customary *levée* and an evening party at Buckingham Palace soon after joining the Foreign Office, took place when I went to Brussels as Third Secretary. There I soon had to accompany my newly arrived chief, Sir George Clerk, when he presented his Letters of Credence to the shy but likeable and greatly respected King Albert. The royal carriages drove into the Embassy courtyard to collect the Ambassador and his suite and conduct us to the Palace and back. When, some thirty years later, I went to present my Credentials to King Albert's grandson I travelled more prosaically by car, though I was escorted by a mounted guard of honour. I also went with George Clerk to Luxembourg where he had similarly to present his Letters to the Grand Duchess, to whom he was accredited as Minister. She, and her family, were very popular, partly because she herself was a person of great charm and distinction, but partly also on account of her courageous behaviour towards the German invaders in the first world war.

* Sir John Russell, until recently Ambassador in Madrid.

My next meeting with King Albert took place skating on the lake at the Royal Palace of Laeken on the outskirts of Brussels, to which members of the foreign diplomatic body had received an open invitation. One of the other skaters was a newly arrived young Swede, who went round introducing himself in the Scandinavian fashion, drawing himself to attention and proclaiming, 'Moi, Schulz'. He eventually went up to a tall figure, who replied, 'Et moi, Roi.'

That winter I attended a Court Ball, an event which was then a normal feature of the social calendar but which is now a very rare occurrence anywhere. The ball was not without incident. The wife of a Balkan diplomat arrived wearing a new Paris creation which the rather stuffy Belgian Court officials decided was indecently décolleté (though I am sure it would not have caused an eyebrow to be raised now) and, protesting bitterly, she was obliged to go and put on a fur wrap—to the delight of some of the other ladies present. At a later stage in the evening the Hungarian Chargé d'Affaires, wearing the romantic uniform of a Magyar nobleman, and having presumably consumed too much royal champagne, drew his curved sword and charged downstairs in pursuit of some imaginary foe.

Very soon after this came the tragic accident when King Albert was killed climbing on the rocks at Marche-les-Dames above the Meuse. Having been involved in a climbing accident myself I was naturally interested in the details. The King, who was an experienced Alpinist, should never, it seemed to me, have risked this climb without a companion and the help of a rope. Moreover, though there are some fine cliffs a little higher up the Meuse above Dinant, on which Belgian climbers are frequently to be seen testing their skill in the summer months, the rocks at Marche-les-Dames always looked to me singularly unattractive.

The funeral of the King was of course a great state occasion, and members of all the royal houses of Europe gathered in Brussels to participate. The Prince of Wales came to represent his father, and I went to dinner at the Embassy to meet him. Lady Clerk, the Ambassadress, was quite a talented painter and persuaded the Prince to sit for his portrait after the dinner guests had departed. When shown the result the Prince was not enthusiastic and commented that he looked very green, which was true enough for Lady

Clerk's choice of colours was rather after Gauguin. Our Vice-Consul, Graham Sebastian, who was also there, had been at Oxford with the Prince and knew him quite well. After dinner the latter was about to accept a glass of whisky when Graham stopped him, saying that he would do much better to stick to the brandy, which was very good, rather than mix the two. Sound advice no doubt, and the Prince meekly followed it, though I thought he looked a trifle surprised.

The funeral was a very long drawn out affair, and though the more junior participants like myself were able to withdraw after the service in the Cathedral and get home in time for a late lunch, the royal mourners all had to proceed in carriages to the crypt at Laeken, several miles away, which meant that they were not liberated until after 3 o'clock. Not only were they very hungry, but they had other problems, and the Prince of Wales gave us a graphic account of how King Boris of Bulgaria at one stage leapt from the carriage which they were sharing, and caused a minor sensation by dashing in full regalia to a street lavatory.

The new King of the Belgians, Leopold III, and Queen Astrid, were a strikingly handsome and charming couple, and she in particular was immensely popular. By the spring of 1935 Court Mourning had at last come to an end and Brussels began to cheer up, aided by a major international exhibition which drew great crowds both from Belgium and from neighbouring countries. One of the outstanding social events was a ball at the British Pavilion and the Duke and Duchess of York came over for the occasion, staying for a couple of nights at the Embassy. Having been presented at the airport I was deputed to escort His Royal Highness when he went to lay a wreath on the tomb of King Albert. The Belgian florist had sprinkled the gigantic wreath very liberally with water, and unfortunately I omitted to give it a shake before handing it to the Duke. As a result he received a minor showerbath, causing momentary and very justifiable irritation. I was on the list of those selected to dance with Queen Astrid at the ball but I was unlucky for just before my turn came the royal party decided that it was time to go home. Only a few months later came the tragic car accident in which she lost her life.

During my period as Private Secretary I was automatically involved in many of the functions during foreign State Visits to

London, or when visiting Foreign Ministers were received at Buckingham Palace. Later, as the Under Secretary in charge of the Foreign Office Protocol Department, I was concerned with the arrangements for foreign representatives at the funeral of King George VI. I was attached for the occasion to the Danish Foreign Minister, Herr Kraft, and walked in the procession from Westminster Hall to Paddington. With various halts en route this took a long time, and being mid-February and decidedly chilly, we were all very glad to get into the special train for Windsor, where refreshments had fortunately been provided. The silent crowds in the streets, the slow-moving procession with the military bands playing an assortment of funeral marches, and finally the service in St George's Chapel, Windsor, combined to make it a memorable occasion.

It was soon time to begin thinking about the arrangements for the Queen's Coronation, and I was appointed to be the Foreign Office representative on the Coronation Executive Committee. The Chairman was the late Duke of Norfolk, who presided with great firmness and competence over this heterogeneous body, which included the Archbishop of Canterbury and many other distinguished personages. The discussions were often animated and we had many unusual problems before us. My chief responsibility was to advise on questions relating to the reception, seating and entertainment of the various foreign potentates and official representatives. To some extent I could be guided by the precedents of the two last Coronations, but much had changed and a good deal of improvisation was necessary. On the strength of my membership of the Committee, Jean and I were allotted seats in the Abbey looking down on the choir-stalls, which gave us an excellent view of all the proceedings. Though we had thought that the many hours which we were obliged to spend there might pass rather slowly, in the event there was so much of interest to see and hear that the period of waiting did not seem long at all. It was, in fact, a wonderfully inspiring occasion and all the careful planning that had preceeded it was amply justified. We also attended the Prime Minister's Coronation Banquet for the Foreign Representatives at Lancaster House and various other such functions. I was made a CVO for my part in the proceedings and would have been made a KCVO had not the Foreign Office said, quite justifiably, that I was too junior for a knighthood. I was destined to become a KCVO later on, at the close of the State Visit to Denmark, and finally, in Brussels, a GCVO.

In the summer of 1952 I had been told that Prince Hussein of Jordan, as he then was, found himself rather unoccupied at Harrow on Sundays, and it was suggested that he would welcome an invitation to spend a day with an English family. He was about the same age as our eldest daughter, and we accordingly invited him to come one Sunday when the girls could be home from school. He was rather shy, but the visit was, I think, enjoyed by all. We had thought that he might have inherited his grandfather, King Abdullah's love of horses, and the ponies had been made ready, but there was the difficulty that his accompanying detective was unable to ride, and anyhow, the Prince appeared to be keener on his newly acquired car than on horses. He took the girls for a drive in order to show off his car's paces. We managed to glean a few items about his impressions of Harrow, and one incident which had clearly given great satisfaction was that his House had defeated at football that of his cousin, the ill-fated young King of Iraq, whose hat he had secured as a trophy in the ensuing celebrations. He wrote a very charming letter of thanks in which he looked forward to 'the match we are so eager to win against the rivel school to ours, Eaton', and sent his best wishes to our eldest daughter, Gillie, for her exams, 'although they don't take Greek which I think still is very boring'. A month or two later he became King. I have continued to watch his eventful career with special sympathy and admiration.

When we arrived in Copenhagen in October 1956 the Danish royal family were in residence at their delightful eighteenth-century country palace of Fredensborg, set in beechwoods to the north of Copenhagen, and it was arranged that I should present my Credentials there. I was escorted by a charming old Lord-in-Waiting, who, by the time we reached the Palace, had invited me to shoot with him a fortnight later. We drove down the motorway at 100 m.p.h. until we got within a mile or two of Fredensborg, when we slowed down to a crawl so as to arrive precisely as the clock struck the appointed hour. A guard of honour was drawn up in the courtyard and a number of colourful figures lined the flight of steps leading up to the front door. As we got out of the car my escort observed in a hoarse whisper, 'The one on your left is a footman but the one on the right is the Lord Chamberlain.' No doubt he had seen some new Ambassador shake hands with the wrong one, and without his prompting I could easily have made the same mistake, for it was difficult to say which was the more splendid.

As a Deputy Under Secretary of State in the Foreign Office I had on several occasions been in attendance when foreign Ambassadors came to present their Credentials to the Queen, and had admired her skill in putting them at their ease. I was assuming that King Frederik would similarly begin our interview with a few words of welcome, but instead he looked at me severely for what seemed rather a long time and then said, 'Well, are you not going to give me your Letters?' It was clear that it was up to me to make the running, so, having duly handed over my Credentials I conveyed messages from the Queen and endeavoured to express in suitable terms my gratification at having been appointed to serve in his friendly and hospitable country. The atmosphere soon became quite easy, and we discussed the Queen's forthcoming visit to Denmark and other topics of mutual interest. With Queen Ingrid the atmosphere was from the outset entirely relaxed and informal.

Planning the Queen's State Visit enabled us to get to know King Frederik and Queen Ingrid rather better than would otherwise have been possible, and we were soon invited to a private lunch *à quatre* in their town Palace in the Amalienborg Square in order to discuss the programme. We then went to inspect the accommodation reserved for royal visitors in one of the other three nearly identical Palaces which look onto the square.

Before we left London we had been told that there were three subjects which the King was happy to discuss—music, ships and his three daughters. He was in fact extremely knowledgeable about music, and as a birthday treat used to conduct the Band of the Royal Guards. Jean and I were not qualified to take him on on that ground, nor were we particularly expert on nautical matters, but having three daughters of our own we could count on at least one happy subject in common. Princess Margrethe, the eldest of the three, and the present Queen of Denmark, was just the same age as our youngest daughter, Davina, who, as a result was invited to various parties at the Palace, while in return Princess Margrethe came several times to balls at the Embassy. She was an enthusiastic dancer of reels, and used also to come with us to the annual ball of the St Andrew's Society of Copenhagen. On one occasion when Davina was staying in a Danish country house on the shore of the Great Belt the royal family arrived in their yacht, and a combined bathing party ensued. As a result she was able to give us a graphic description of the tattoos on the royal sailor's chest.

A State Visit calls for a great deal of detailed preparatory work by the Embassy on the spot, and I soon found myself increasingly involved. Visits to some of the remoter countries are doubtless more exciting than those to countries like Denmark and Belgium with which relations are anyhow extremely close. Nevertheless, in my experience, such visits give very great pleasure in the receiving country, and they provide an occasion for demonstrating and celebrating mutual friendship and common interests. Assuming that the timing is favourable, by which I mean that there are no pressing contentious issues which are likely to sour the atmosphere, there should be benefits to both countries. The visits are of course exhausting affairs for the principal participants, since it is scarcely possible to prevent the programme from being a very full one. The Queen and Prince Philip certainly do all that is expected of them and a bit more, and given the limits imposed by security, which must always be a problem, it is difficult to see how one could improve on the present technique.

The Queen arrived in Copenhagen in the royal yacht and it had been arranged that I should go on board when she was off Elsinore. The approach by water is undoubtedly the ideal way to arrive in Copenhagen—the same is true of New York—and standing on the bridge with the Queen as we sailed down the Sound and into the splendid harbour I was able to point out some of the principal sights. The presence of the royal yacht during the visit meant, incidentally, that the Queen's banquet for the King and Queen of Denmark was given on board and not at the Embassy. This was in some ways a relief, though of course we still had a good deal to do with the planning of the evening.

On the first morning of the visit the Queen came to the Embassy, where members of the staff and their wives were presented to her, as well as our three daughters and our son Joe who had got away from school for the occasion. Prince Philip commiserated with him on having three older sisters. While the party was in progress one of our dachshunds decided that the right place for her to be was as near to the Queen as possible, and accordingly went and sat at her feet, to the amusement of all concerned.

The other main events followed the normal pattern for such visits—state banquet, gala performance at the Opera, reception for the British and Commonwealth communities, and so on, one exception being a visit to the house of Professor Niels Bohr, the distinguished atomic scientist. He was a very charming old man who rather surprisingly led a most active social life, so that we often met him dining out. He had many interesting stories to tell of his wartime experiences, and of encounters with Churchill, Roosevelt and others. Unfortunately, though his English was very good, he spoke in such a soft voice that it was very difficult to hear what he said. One story which he told against himself and which I did manage to catch related to a top secret trip to the United States in I think 1942. By chance he was spotted in New York by a Danish acquaintance who hailed him and said loudly, 'Fancy meeting you here, Professor Bohr.' The Professor, remembering his briefing, replied severely, 'I think you must be mistaken,' but spoilt the effect by adding as an afterthought, 'But do tell me, how is your Uncle Hans?'

The Danes must be unrivalled in their enthusiasm for celebrating birthdays, even those of fairly distant relations. 'I am sorry I cannot come—you see it is my great aunt's seventy-fifth birthday' was the sort of reply one quite often received. All such occasions are the pretext for a family gathering—and the Danes are quick to accept any suggestion for a party. When, before my departure for Copenhagen, I asked the Danish Ambassador in London whether the Danes had any preferences as regards wine, e.g. claret as opposed to Burgundy, or German rather than French white wines, he gave me the following sound advice, 'All Danes like drinking other peoples' wine.' But if they could choose what it should be they would almost certainly opt for claret. Failing this a combination of schnapps and Tuborg (or Carlsberg) was an acceptable answer on many occasions.

My fiftieth birthday occurred while we were in Copenhagen but this I did not reveal to our Danish friends. On the other hand our Silver Wedding clearly was an occasion for a party and we decided

L

to give a ball. The Copenhagen Embassy ballroom, all white and gold, is the finest room in the house, and with the adjoining series of drawing rooms is well suited to a party on a considerable scale. Perhaps the outstanding feature of this particular evening was the flowers. It is the pleasant Danish custom to send flowers on all such occasions and bouquets began arriving from all our Danish friends, from the King and Queen and Princess Margrethe downwards, till the whole house was bedecked. The guests were a mixture of generations but this did not prevent the party being a great success.

The Queen's visit to Belgium in May 1966 was, rather surprisingly, the first by a British Sovereign for forty-four years, and the Belgians were determined to make the most of it. Planning the programme was more complicated than in Denmark, since, as always in Belgium, it was necessary to preserve a fair balance between the Walloon and Flemish parts of the country, which meant that if the Queen was going to Antwerp she must also go to Liège. Bruges and Ypres clearly deserved to be included and the French-speaking south got a second innings when the Queen and Prince Philip went to spend a night at the royal château of Ciergnon in the Ardennes. There they were able to drive out into the forest in the evening and to see wild boar and other animals.

Belgium is of course covered in battlefields on very many of which the British have played a major rôle. There are those of the campaigns of Marlborough like Ramillies and Oudenarde, and of course Waterloo and Quatre Bras, Ypres and Paschendaele, Zeebrugge and Antwerp. The State Visit was hardly an occasion for a round of battlefields and we deliberately kept away from Waterloo, but the British contribution to the defence and liberation of Belgium in the two world wars was inevitably a main theme throughout the visit of almost every Belgian speaker—and there were a good many of them. The afternoon in Ypres, where British military bands performed in the Grand' Place and where the Last Post and Reveille were sounded at the Menin Gate, provided a moving finale to the whole visit.

One awkward problem was what to do about King Leopold and his wife, Princess Liliane, who, though they lived close to Brussels, were completely excluded from all official functions. It was finally agreed that the Queen should go to tea with them privately on her way back from Liège, and this seemed to meet with general approval. It is sad that the former King, who has so many qualities and such unusual charm, should, since his abdication, have been unable to find any useful rôle.

The return dinner party given by the Queen and Prince Philip for the King and Queen of the Belgians, together with the Prince and Princess of Liège, was this time to take place at the Embassy. By careful planning and additions to the table and by taking the doors off their hinges it was possible at a pinch to seat about fifty people in our dining room. The dinner was quite a test both for our chef and for our young and not particularly experienced Spanish butler, who had to be in charge of the operations, though he had assistance from various distinguished characters from Buckingham Palace such as the Yeoman of the Silver Pantry and the Queen's Page. In the event, all went without a hitch and both the food and the wine, which was of course my responsibility, were, I think, worthy of the occasion. The Embassy was quite well supplied with silver, including a fine set of plates which had originally been made for the Embassy at Vienna in the 1820s— before Belgium was an independent country—but these were not used as a complete supply of silver, china and glass, which Jean and I had been allowed to select, had been brought from Buckingham Palace. The dining room, and indeed all the main rooms of the house which were in use that evening, formed a fine setting for the dinner and for the large reception which followed it. Here I had my work cut out trying to ensure that the most deserving rather than the most pushing were presented to the Queen.

One minor problem which had provoked some discussion beforehand was our lift. This was extremely elegant but it had been known to stick and it could only accommodate three people. Supposing the Queens decided to go upstairs in it, could one risk letting them both be stuck together? And anyhow whose lady-in-waiting should accompany them, or should it be the Ambassadress? In the event, though we had taken the precaution of having an expert in the building, the lift was not used.

Several Belgians remarked during the visit on the easy and relaxed relationship between the Queen and Prince Philip and members of their staff. The Belgian Court has a tradition of greater formality, and the King and Queen are made to appear more remote, though this is certainly not the fault of King Baudouin or

Queen Fabiola, both of whom are very accessible. One Belgian observed to me after the visit was over—and he intended it as a compliment—that I appeared to treat the Queen as if she were my sister. I hope I did not overdo the informality, but if so I expect it was a fault on the right side.

One feature that struck many of us during the visit was the exceptional popularity of Queen Fabiola. This is in no way surprising as she looks charming, has a very engaging and friendly manner and in addition to talking many languages almost perfectly, including of course Flemish as well as French and English (not to mention her native Spanish) is so obviously a perfect companion to the King, himself a man of many parts. I always found Queen Fabiola very easy to talk to, much more so than her sister-in-law, Princess Paola, who always looked beautiful and was very well dressed but who was not the most forthcoming table companion.

One of the occasions during the State Visit which we most enjoyed was when we, together with the three children we had with us (Gillie, Susan and Joe) were unexpectedly invited to go back, after the gala performance at the Opera, to an informal supper with the royal party in the flood-lit greenhouses at Laeken which contain many magnificent trees and shrubs from the Congo and of which the King was justifiably proud.

In the course of our stay in Brussels we also had visits from Princess Margaret and Lord Snowdon, the Duke and Duchess of Kent, and Princess Marina (for the funeral of the old Queen Elisabeth, King Albert's widow).

The Duke and Duchess of Kent came to stay for the week of ceremonies which commemorated the 150th anniversary of the Battle of Waterloo. When I arrived in Brussels in the summer of 1963 there was already some discussion on what would be the most appropriate way of marking the occasion. It was clear that it would be a mistake to lay too much stress on Waterloo as a great British victory and that we should rather seek to commemorate it as a turning point in the history of Europe. Not only was it desirable to avoid unnecessary offence to French susceptibilities but we had to remember that there had been about an equal number of Belgians fighting on each side, and there were still certain Walloon societies which regarded the defeat of Napoleon as a disaster for Belgium, leading as it did to a period when the country passed under Dutch rule.

It was finally agreed that the main events of the programme should be a memorial service on the battlefield, in the grounds of the farm of Hougomont, on the morning of 18 June, a display given by thirteen British military bands the following night, and a ball at the Embassy on 15 June, the exact anniversary of the historic party given by the Duchess of Richmond on the eve of the preliminary battles of Quatre Bras and Ligny (not of Waterloo itself as Byron would have us believe). There were other supporting events such as a film gala in aid of the British Charitable Fund, which was founded shortly after the battle of Waterloo in order to help the wounded and the dependants of those who had lost their lives in the battle, and which still looks after the sick and elderly members of the British community in Belgium. Then, since the Duke of Richmond had organised a cricket match for British officers a few days before his wife's ball, it seemed appropriate to arrange a match now, and the Brussels club took on the Household Brigade in a game which ended, amid much excitement, in a tie. I myself planted a commemorative oak tree on what is still known as the Pelouse des Anglais in the Bois de la Cambre, where the original game is reputed to have taken place.

Rather surprisingly, Monsieur Spaak, as mentioned previously, was very dubious of the wisdom of our plans, and chose not to participate in any of the events of the week, though he subsequently admitted that he thought this had been an error of judgment. There certainly seemed to be very few of his countrymen, official or otherwise, who shared his hesitation. It was less surprising to find that the French Embassy, reputedly on the personal instructions of General de Gaulle, not only elected to take no part whatever in the proceedings, but even made use of one of the French-language Brussels newspapers to criticise and try to pour cold water on the whole affair. At one stage they reported that we had run into such difficulties that the ball was to be cancelled, while a little later on it was announced that the French Ambassador had after all decided not to press me to call it off!

The Germans and the Dutch had from the outset shown much interest in our plans and wished to be associated with the commemorative ceremonies. Among our German guests was Prince

Ernst, Duke of Brunswick, whose ancestor had been present at the original ball and is said to have had a premonition of his approaching end—he was killed next day at Quatre Bras. The German and Dutch Ambassadors were of course also invited to the ball, as well as those of the other countries which had been allies or associates in the final campaign against Napoleon, including the Austrians, Portuguese and Scandinavians. The Commonwealth Ambassadors also took a keen interest in our plans and they were all naturally included.

The memorial service at Hougomont was organised with great care and efficiency by the British military authorities who arranged for a detachment to be present from each of the Waterloo regiments, making about a thousand men in all. It was an impressive occasion, and the violent rainstorm which soaked most of those present (of whom Wellington's brilliant biographer, Lady Longford, was one) was not altogether inappropriate as it recalled the conditions on the eve of the battle itself.

The event with which we personally were most concerned and which had called for much careful planning over a long period, was naturally the ball at the Embassy. So far as possible we endeavoured to emphasise the links with the Duchess of Richmond's ball, which, owing to its dramatic timing and to the fascination it has exercised on poets and writers from Byron onwards, is, I suppose, one of the best known social events in our history. The Duke of Richmond very kindly lent us the manuscript list of guests who had been invited to the original ball, and this we had on view for the evening as well as some fine pieces of furniture from the original ballroom. (The house in the rue de la Blanchisserie where the Duchess's ball took place has long since been pulled down, though it is possible to identify its approximate location.) We made a point of inviting representatives of as many as possible of the Belgian families whose ancestors had been at the original ball, and there were also quite a few on the British side, beginning with the then Duke of Wellington, his son and daughter-in-law (the present Duke and Duchess) and his grandson. The Duke and Duchess of Richmond were unfortunately unable to come but the family were well represented by Lord and Lady Nicholas Gordon-Lennox.

We received a great deal of assistance and advice from the late General Sir William Stirling, the Commander-in-Chief of BAOR and the British military authorities in Germany. They helped us to arrange that at least one couple representing each of the forty-odd Waterloo regiments should receive invitations, and many other distinguished soldiers, including Field Marshals Templer and Hull, were also present. We had trumpeters to sound a fanfare on the arrival of the more eminent guests, and pipers to play for the Scottish dancing, which had also been a feature of the original ball. In the course of the evening Robert Speaight recited the famous verses from Byron's 'Childe Harold', which helped to contribute to the sense of history of which many people were, I think, conscious.

The Brussels Embassy is a fine house and has several good rooms, but the very decorative ballroom on the first floor was by no means large enough for a party on this scale. Accordingly a dance floor was laid in the courtyard which was completely covered in and decorated for the occasion, and this, together with the candle-lit ballroom, provided ample room for dancing. The great assortment of military uniforms, foreign as well as British, helped to make it a brilliant scene. A few of the guests came in costume of the period. I had borrowed the now obsolete full dress ambassadorial uniform coat to wear with my white breeches and silk stockings, which seemed more suitable for the occasion than my own more modern and less decorative version.

All the five hundred and fifty guests had been included in dinner parties given either at other Embassies or by Belgian friends, so that all present had met a number of fellow guests before they arrived, and from the outset the party went with a great swing. The King and Queen of the Belgians were abroad at the time but the guests included the Prince de Liège and Princess Paola as well as the Duke and Duchess of Kent and Prince Michael of Kent, all of whom appeared to enjoy themselves as much as everyone else. We were quite sorry when the time came to bring the party to an end. It was undoubtedly the most spectacular social event that took place in Brussels during our time there, and there had been nothing like it for many years previously, nor, I suspect, has there been since. It was certainly the most successful party we ever gave. We naturally had plenty of enthusiastic letters afterwards, and several writers said they doubted whether the original party had been nearly as splendid or as well organised. This may well be true but then the Duchess of Richmond doubtless had problems which did not confront us, and there was certainly no sudden exodus from our party!

Some months before the anniversary celebrations I had got the Duke of Wellington, Lord Anglesey and Field Marshals Templar and Hull to join with me in writing a letter to *The Times* appealing for contributions towards the cost of restoring the so-called Chapelle Royale which forms the entrance to the village church at Waterloo and contains many memorials to those who lost their lives in the battle, and also towards the improvement of the Wellington Museum. This is housed in the old building almost opposite the church where Wellington spent the night after the battle and wrote his despatch describing the outcome of the day. In our letter we quoted his famous comment: 'It gives me the greatest satisfaction to assure Your Lordship that the army never, on any occasion, conducted itself better.' Our appeal met with quite a satisfactory response, and with generous assistance from the Belgian authorities the chapel was restored and redecorated. The Central Office of Information helped to expand and improve the Wellington Museum, which is now a great deal more interesting than it was before 1965, and is certainly well worth a visit. It is a pity that so many tourists, particularly those in coaches, are not made aware of its existence and are taken straight to the great mound surmounted by a lion which dominates the battlefield and to the Panorama in a building below it which gives a colourful but rather French-slanted impression of the battle. The adjoining souvenir shops appear to be interested only in Napoleon and the uninformed tourist might well go away assuming that he had been the victor. The great Duke, incidentally, is reported to have been much incensed by the erection of the mound, remarking that 'They have spoilt my battlefield.' No doubt it made it all look rather different to him and among other things the famous sunken road was largely obliterated, but nevertheless Waterloo still remains one of the least changed of all great battlefields.

By the time we left Brussels I had become something of an expert on the battle and its literature. We knew the whole area pretty well, partly as a result of conducting many visitors there and partly because a part of the battlefield was one of our favourite places for a walk. From time to time it is threatened with new roads or even motorways, but the Embassy keeps a watchful eye on all such projects and it is to be hoped that it will continue to be preserved from any major encroachment.

If Waterloo was the most spectacular and most discussed of the various anniversaries which took place during our time in Brussels, it was far from being the only one. We had the fiftieth anniversary of the battles of Ypres, which were also duly commemorated—and at which I had to make a fairly carefully worded speech as German representatives were present. Then we had Zeebrugge, for which Lord Mountbatten and a shipload of survivors of the raid came over. A ceremony on the quayside was followed by a luncheon party on one of HM ships at which Mountbatten produced a wonderful selection of stories of Churchill and other wartime leaders, which greatly delighted the Prince de Liège. The twenty-fifth anniversary of the Battle of Britain was duly commemorated in Brussels, and we took the opportunity to entertain all those Belgians who had fought with the RAF. Other great events of the last war, such as the Normandy landings, were not forgotten, and the various Belgian Resistance organisations also had a series of dates which had to be celebrated in some way.

Our 'British Week' in 1967 was a major undertaking for the Embassy. Princess Margaret was to have inaugurated it but was unfortunately unwell at the critical moment and Lord Snowdon came on in advance. There was much to interest him in the various exhibitions and displays, and the only problem was to try to ensure that his enthusiasm did not cause us to fall too far behind schedule. Princess Margaret was fortunately able to fly out in time to participate in the later events.

The week was a spectacular success from the general standpoint of Anglo-Belgian relations. It was more difficult to assess whether the commercial results were such as to justify the very considerable amount of time and money which had gone into the preparations, but taking a long view I am confident that it was all worth while. It was a strenuous time for Jean and myself—the peak period covered considerably more than a week—and there was a concentrated programme of social, cultural and sporting engagements, including a series of parties at the Embassy. I found myself opening dress-shows, drawing the first pint at several British pubs and making at least two speeches a day in assorted languages, including

L*

usually a section in Flemish. Whitbreads had brought over for the occasion a dray drawn by two splendid Shires, named, if I remember right, Hengist and Horsa. This drew up, by arrangement, in front of the Embassy, and Jean then drove it round the Parc Royal. An Ambassadress driving a brewer's dray with ease and assurance was, to say the least, an unusual sight and I question whether there are any other Ambassadresses today who are capable of driving a pair of horses.

The Belgians, like the Danes, love wearing decorations, and the more the merrier. I am old-fashioned enough to think that when a special party is given in a glamorous setting like an Embassy in a major capital, and when the ladies put on their best, there is something to be said for the men appearing in the rapidly vanishing attire of tail coats, white ties and decorations. The modern combination of dinner jackets and decorations always looks to me particularly unsmart. I dare say that diplomatic uniforms themselves will not survive much longer, in which case the only males to contribute a little variety and colour to future diplomatic occasions will be some of the African or Middle Eastern representatives who appear in their national dress.

These sartorial comments are not meant to be taken too seriously, and of course an Ernie Bevin or a Winston Churchill can wear what he likes anywhere and get away with it. But there is perhaps a tendency for lesser British politicians to pay insufficient regard to the social customs and conventions of countries they visit. Other Western Europeans in general tend to be more formal and more strict in their observance of such conventions than the casual British, who are liable to cause surprise and even offence by their apparent disregard of them. An obvious example is the seating arrangements at table, which are considered of much greater significance in many foreign countries than they are here.

The whole of this chapter, and indeed much of this book, may sound a bit old-fashioned to my grandchildren. They will doubtless think it quaint that on occasion I used to appear in uniform coat, white knee breeches and silk stockings. I rather doubt whether any present British Ambassador even possesses them, and I do not suppose that anyone will wear them at the next Coronation as I did at the last.

I realise, too, that this chapter with its emphasis on royal connections and brilliant social functions, may have given a rather misleading impression of modern diplomatic life. There are not now many capitals like Brussels, or for that matter Copenhagen, and diplomats in say Vientiane or Bagdad, Sofia or Brazzaville have to live in very different style. In Kinshasa one may go out to dinner at an Embassy without putting on a tie of any kind— and quite right too in that climate. It is in any case an offence for a Zaïrois to wear such an 'un-authentic' item of dress as a tie.

If in our final spell in Brussels we enjoyed some of the more sophisticated amenities of a diplomatic way of life which is tending to disappear it was perhaps to some extent a compensation for earlier periods of intense activity, in particular during the fifteen years from 1936 onwards which culminated in my very exacting spell as Private Secretary. I hope in any case that I have not given the impression that we were unduly impressed by the superficial trappings of ambassadorial existence. It had been fine while it lasted to have a butler come in to announce dinner with a deferential 'Madame l'Ambassadrice est servie', but we both rather liked the system we evolved after our return home under which Jean would despatch from the kitchen her spaniel bearing in her mouth a piece of paper which she would proudly present to me and on which was written the one word 'come'.

INDEX